BOOKED OUT!

Susan Lee

BOOKED OUT!

How to Start and Grow a Successful Regional Tourism Business

Susan Lee

Endorsements

> Booked Out! is an incredibly comprehensive and cohesive journey through the must-knows of developing a tourism enterprise and setting a course for business growth. Susan has generously brought to this practical guide her vast lived experience and professional industry skills and knowledge for the reader to benefit from, whilst also making it an easy read with actionable learnings every step of the way.

Liz Ward (her/she)
Co-founder and CEO
Tourism Tribe

> This book is just what the industry needs right now. It is going to help so many people, from old school tourism operators who have been in the industry for years trying to shake things up to engage new clientele, to people trying to break into the industry and don't fully understand how the beast works.
>
> Susan mentored me as an up and coming Aboriginal tourism operator, she helped me streamline my operations and think outside of the box when it came to engaging different markets. She has a wealth of knowledge and amazing respect for how different peoples and cultures can benefit from working in the industry, without compromising and damaging culture and community relationships.
>
> Her guidance and positive support really helped me grow as a business owner, gain traction and create a brand that is now well known across the tourism industry.

Juan Walker
Owner/Operator
Walkabout Cultural Adventures

Booked Out! is a must-read for aspiring tourism entrepreneurs, offering essential guidance for those planning to offer accommodation, tours or attractions in regional Australia. With practical advice based on insights from experienced operators this book provides a comprehensive understanding of the industry's fundamentals, strategies, and tactics. It's an easy to read indispensable tool for navigating the complexities of the sector and building a profitable business. Whether you're new to regional tourism or have some experience, this book is an essential read for anyone looking to succeed in the tourism industry.

Ben Law
The Financial Bloke podcast

This book is truly valuable and I wish back in the day I had such a resource.

Karen Ellis
Director
Camel Treks Australia

Susan is a fearless professional who tells it how it is. Her knowledge, thoughtfulness and hard work has seen her deliver outstanding outcomes for business and tourism destinations across the country. One of her best capacities is to derive insight where others can't. Booked Out! provides a wonderful overview of our industry and is a fantastic asset for new tourism businesses.

Shaun de Bruyn
CEO
Tourism Industry Council of SA

I first went into a tourism business over 40 years ago and I wish I had a guide book like this to help me when I first began. Tourism is a specialised business and in some ways works the opposite to many other businesses. A good understanding before you make those first steps will vastly improve your chances of success. I recommend this book to all thinking of joining the industry.

Rod Quartermain
Chairman
Australia's Golden Outback, WA

This book is a great resource for anyone on the land considering starting a tourism business as well as those in government working with operators to fully realise local and regional economic opportunities. Pragmatic, fun and easy to read, Booked Out! makes the case for why strong, profitable businesses are essential to sustain Australia's regional advantage, and to do so by tapping into low hanging fruit such as self-drive markets, the bread and butter of so many regions.

Sean G Holden
CEO
Local Government Association NT

Booked Out! How to Start and Grow a Successful Regional Tourism Business

First printing 2023

ISBN: 978-0-9756415-1-4

Publishing: CVC Clear Vision Consulting
Editer: Clare Wadsworth
Design: Rasika Um, shashika.info
Front cover image: clockwise from right: Stockphoto, Camel Trek Australia Pty Ltd, Lost Retreats, Lost in Mt Jagged, Lakeside Retreat
Back cover image: by Heidi Wolff Photography

Taveller's Lifecycle diagram from https://medium.com/@giannisgeorgiadis/tourism-within-mobile-technology-c93f1c908d20

ACKNOWLEDGEMENT OF COUNTRY

I pay my respects to and acknowledge Aboriginal and Torres Strait Islander people, Elders and ancestors across Australia.

May we share a positive future together.

This book is dedicated to my clients and mentors.

CLEAR VISION CONSULTING

Strategy / Planning / Marketing / Growth

www.cvconsult.com.au

Wooleen Station, Murchison, Tourism Western Australia

CONTENTS

CHAPTER 6 - DESTINATIONS, PRODUCTS, EXPERIENCES

CHAPTER 7 - REGIONAL CHARACTERISTICS

CHAPTER 8 - BECOMING AN OPERATOR

CHAPTER 9 - CAN I REALLY MAKE MONEY FROM THAT?

CHAPTER 10 - REGIONAL TOURISM BUSINESS FUNDAMENTALS

Boat on the Tamar, Launceston, Tasmania. Brand Tasmania

INTRODUCTION

Who is this book for?

This book is for budding micro/small business owners starting out in tourism - whether you're setting up a small enterprise in accommodation, an attraction or tours.

You're probably looking to make some money from a special or unique experience, wanting to turn an existing asset like a house, shed, bus or gallery into an income-generating side business, or moving beyond a hobby, but are unsure of where to start, what to do in what order, how much to invest, and how to promote it. You probably have practical skills, some time and are willing to learn, but you're completely new to regional tourism, don't know what you don't know, and haven't got a network of people to seek advice from.

Why this book?

You can fast track your success in a number of ways, and you've taken the first step by buying and reading this book. **Booked Out!** will guide you through transitioning from weekend hobbyist to industry operator with confidence and pride.

My early research showed there are a lot of 'how to get rich quick under 30' books already available and, given most of us aren't under 30 or rich, that tells you something about their insights. Author Toni Morrison said "If there's a book that you want to read, but it hasn't been written yet, then you must write it." And this is what I've done.

I've coached hundreds of people starting up in tourism, and business owners diversifying by using a tourism marketing strategy to promote their service. I've seen first-hand how quickly people get overwhelmed with advice often conflicting and from many perspectives – given by people who have zero experience in business, no regional visitor experiences, and no skin in the game.

Two of the many questions I am often asked are "How can I afford to transition from my job into a regional tourism owner?" and "How do I market my business to get bookings fast?"

The perception is that starting and marketing a regional tourism business is easy - just like starting any business, but tourism and regional. This simply isn't the case. Building a regional tourism business is way more than just marketing. It's complicated by a myriad of other factors such as your day job and family commitments, your budget, travel plans, language barriers, registrations, disability requirements, cultural differences, the area you are in, how close to airports/cities you are, seasons, other local tourism offerings - and the list goes on.

Booked Out! focuses on all of these and more, and will help you to get started, become informed, direct your research, and shine a light on the key things to consider to get the most bang for your buck.

Booked Out!:

- shows you how to bootstrap (that is build it and grow it sale by sale, reinvesting profits to grow) your regional tourism (ad)venture
- outlines tourism business fundamentals, strategies and tactics that have worked for other operators

- covers the regional context in which many tourism businesses operate, explaining the various layers in tourism that will help draw visitors to your place or town

- focuses on planning, starting, and operating a sustained, profitable business, and maybe even setting up passive income (yes, you can make money operating a regional business at arm's length with a few secret weapons on hand)

- highlights the specific challenges regional operators face, and also some of the benefits of being removed from city-centric support and competitors

- provides tips on marketing on a shoestring, and the different considerations for different product types and business size

- shares some of the tools, platforms, resources and distribution systems available to you on a budget

Booked Out! is easy to follow. In some cases I show what going to the next level looks like so you can start to see the bigger picture - though I don't suggest you need to go there at once, or at all! I encourage you to work within your capacity or just at the edge of it, where you are being challenged and mastering fundamental new skills - but slowly and patiently so that you can develop the internal confidence to take risks and implement new plans.

How to use this book

Think of this book as your own personal coach. When you encounter bumps on the road, you can look them up and get advice and insights on how to deal with them. They're probably more common than you think, and there are ways for business owners new to tourism to navigate them. You're not alone.

Each chapter begins with an overview and ends with a recap of key points. Key resources are also highlighted at the end of the book.

So, if you want to start a tourism business, if you have an idea, go right ahead. This book is for you, whoever you are, wherever you are. You can absolutely do it, and you will give value and get value from offering relief, respite, bad jokes, good wine, a comfortable bed - forms of grace - to travellers in your part of the world.

My hope is that this book will make the early stages of planning your business a little easier as you gain tourism knowledge, take considered risks, and grow bookings using your own capital, smarts and opportunities. You never know what people are interested in doing, seeing or experiencing while on holiday!

After reading this book I hope you will be inspired, armed with knowledge, and motivated to set out to do something that may have been sitting in your 'one day' pile.

Maybe one day is today.

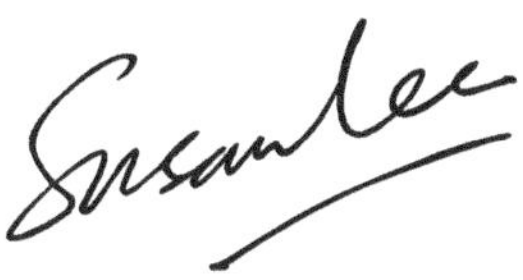

Mountain biking, Victoria's High Country. Visit Victoria

CHAPTER ONE

GETTING STARTED

WHY REGIONAL TOURISM?

Regions are where our great cultural and natural stories are, where our archaeology and geology are still intact in vast tracts of land, where our critters and flora, our mountains and forests and coastlines, islands, lakes and rivers are, and they are all connected to our food and wine, agriculture, and people. This is what people come to Australia for. To see our vast landscapes, and appreciate 60,000-year-old Indigenous cultural connections, the oldest continuous culture in the world. Just to get a taste of it, people travel far and wide to experience a little piece of an authentic Australia. It's valuable and we should talk about it, fight for it, and be proud of it. Our national brand is not in our cities; it's in how the regions and the country are perceived, for better or for worse.

One size fits all advice simply does not work in Australian regional tourism, and although there are common issues, there may be different solutions. Some regions are more popular than others, depending on geography, weather and seasonality, population, access, cultural events and activities, whether a celebrity has endorsed it, worked or lives there (this might turn a lot of visitors off too!).

Your town may be known for something like films being made there, or for a particular cultural event like the Diwali Regional Food Festival, or National Sheep Dog Trials, or the craft of making beanies as is the case in Alice Springs. Other factors include proximity to major tourism access points such as airports, harbours, train stations, and also the kinds of experiences and infrastructure on offer. Having cycle trails, being known for something, is a draw card for visitors, and helps regions to start to build critical mass around attractions like national parks, unique sights, and experiences such as trips on the water, oyster tasting, and underground accommodation.

Regional business owners need help to grow and fully realise their potential in a sustainable, appropriate way. Regions are where a lot of Australia's nature-based experiences occur, and Tourism Australia research consistently shows this is what visitors to Australia and within Australia want to participate in. This is even increasing as awareness of the impact of environmental issues and climate change is felt worldwide - people are valuing nature more highly as we slowly acknowledge its rapid changes due to man-made repercussions and emissions. People also want to visit places with solutions to these problems. And Australia, paradoxically, while a big global emitter, also holds key answers, often in regions with natural resources and renewables where approaches are innovative.

One of the challenges of regional tourism is that research shows most international visitors to Australia rarely travel into regions; they stick to the city they fly into and visit areas a day's trip from capital cities, mostly Sydney and Melbourne. So there is a huge untapped opportunity for regions to showcase their strengths and experiences to draw visitors out of cities.

International visitor spending in regions is incredibly valuable as it is rare, expensive to attract, and, as COVID 19 showed us, was income sorely missed by many regional businesses which had to find new markets or close their doors due to international travel restrictions. The reality is, Australia is a huge country, and most first-time visitors have no conception of the vastness of our landscape and the distances between towns, cities, natural wonders, and man-made experiences. Those who do visit regions for holidays are specifically seeking nature or a particular experience, and will take a tour or drive themselves if there are no direct flights.

Regions suffer from brain drain as skilled young people leave country towns and surrounding communities to seek job opportunities in cities. Tourism, as it scales, can provide more local economic benefit than the mining and resources sector, where salaries are spent back in big cities or overseas by fly-in, fly-out (FIFO) workers.

In regions, there are local guardians of places, landowners, and custodians of the country with stories to share, not least Australia's First Nations people and traditional owners, but also multi-generational farmers and their families, who may be looking to diversify, to drought-proof their farm income with tourism. Supporting and growing regional tourism is a way of preserving the communities that give places their unique character and feel, and visitors a special adventure. You remember the character of the Blue Mountains or the Daintree by the people you meet.

What are tourism regions?

The Fleurieu, the Gold Coast, the Kimberley - these are tourism regions. No two regions across Australia are the same. Australia has 77 tourism regions, according to Tourism Research Australia (TRA). These are defined in consultation with state/territory tourism organizations, and often reflect a grouping of local government boundaries. ACT has one region, and Victoria has twenty-one, so you can see how each state differs - and Tourism Australia's dilemma in featuring all regions in international campaigns. It's just not possible!

To learn more about regions, and which region you are in, visit Tourism Research Australia's website (see details in the Resources section at the back of this book). TRA publish Regional Tourism Profiles quarterly and annually, and these Australian tourism region data profiles are excellent resources for business planning, and learning your regions' market characteristics if you are a new operator.

Regional Tourism Profiles give data on:

- tourism visitors, nights and spend
- purpose of visit
- activities visitors take part in in the region
- domestic and international markets
- tourism employment
- tourism businesses
- accommodation
- aviation

You would be ahead of many people, just by learning the visitor information of your region. Knowing these facts and figures helps if you want to apply for grants later on, but mainly it helps in planning your marketing strategy to attract visitors. For example, you may decide to start exporting (selling to international visitors before they arrive in Australia), earlier if your region has a high number of international visitors who really want what you have to offer. This will fundamentally change your marketing and pricing strategy from day one.

SMALL IS BEAUTIFUL

All of the great journey stories - The Odyssey, The Lord of the Rings, Star Wars, Thelma and Louise, the New Testament – ok, you get it... the main characters travel a lot. But while they seek refuge from armies, try to win their wives back, sail past sexy hussies, wrestle golden jewellery from goblins, collect new disciples, and outrun the cops, they still need transport, shelter, food, company, directions, companionship, and the odd souvenir (Wookie mug, anyone?).

My point is, hospitality is fundamentally a service industry that has evolved from a basic bed, night and meal to Instagrammable experiences by influencers on elaborate adventures to very cool places. It's become aspirational for many, a status symbol. But while travel is an escape to some, it's a necessity for others, a chore, part of a job, or a regular vacation. There's now a wide range of what constitutes tourism, and there's probably a place for your idea if you can find enough people to book you in a region that is stable enough to support tourism.

Travel has become fashionable, and can be a little intimidating if you are considering starting a new regional tourism business. Marketing does feature larger, established businesses, because they are often more invested, but small business has its place, and offers the diversity of things to see and do that all successful tourism regions need. Most tourism businesses in Australia are small - micro even. Not everyone stays in large hotels - look at the boom of Airbnb as consumers actively seek alternatives, and can now visit lesser-known places because people have opened up their homes as hosts where perhaps before there were limited accommodation options. Small is beautiful and, as Paul Kelly sings, from little things, big things grow. I wrote this book because, at some point in your journey, your regional tourism business idea may not fit in with government campaigns, business programs, grants, or even the regional tourism brand. This may leave you wondering if you need to fit in to be successful - and there are a whole host of other myths. Let's look at some of these common misbeliefs now.

Myth busting

I won't make money unless I'm a big business

You can do very well as a small business, but success does not mean the same thing to everyone, so decide early what it looks like for you. Is it about earnings? Is your idea of success being booked out? It's easy to feel intimidated by established operators, but TRA research shows most tourism businesses (95%) are micro and small to medium (SME), run by individuals or partnerships. Most earn under $200,000 a year (more like $50,000 in 2021). Being a small regional tourism business is a great way to start because you can diversify quickly in the face of change or competition, and can raise margins with less cost if set up right. A small business is an excellent training ground, and can evolve into a medium (over 19 employees) or large (over 50 employees) business by scaling later if you set it up early on.

It seems like all the attention, support and focus is on marketing large, established tourism businesses

There's no doubt big business is heavily invested, employs a lot of people, and pays a lot of tax so has more sway and power, but in Australia more people travel economy than first class, and more people can afford to stay in cabins and caravan parks than in high-end hotels. Anyone can be - and is - in tourism. Look around!

Small operators often report feeling excluded from opportunities or believe it is implied that as a small business they are not worthy of help, attention or support - not a fit for state marketing campaigns, not eligible for grants, and they are told they are 'not ready'. Sadly, government is not great at working with small, diverse businesses or tailoring policy for different communities. You may encounter this, so just be ready to find your own way of succeeding independently of the government.

I'll never make the Top 10 Travel experiences lists

'Top 10 Best of...' lists are marketing tools developed to simplify things, and used to raise a profile and attract attention to a region. You can be very successful in a small business, and tap into a niche market in your local area, and provide a lot of value to visitors as well as the region you operate in without being on the must-do lists in your state or region.

But if you are on a Top 10 list for your region or have the chance to be on it, jump at it as it will give you great exposure. If there isn't one in your region - why not simply create one, put your business on it and market it?

Don't they know who I am? I should be getting more exposure.

Easy, tiger! Objectivity is important when you start out, so don't expect to be featured and supported in ways that may not be appropriate for your business size, age or stage. I've seen tourism operators become very agitated when they don't get the attention they feel they deserve from the media, government campaigns or regional tourism marketing bodies. But as the saying goes, you get more bees with honey than vinegar. Also, if you are making money without being featured on the front of the Visitor Guide, does it really matter? You've got all that to look forward to!

Being under the radar is not a bad place if you already have bookings and a market. I know one camel safari operator (featured on the cover of this book) who rarely did any marketing as she had full occupancy and a repeat market paying $3,000 a trip. Although she barely got a mention in the region's Top 10 things to do, she went on to win a state Tourism Award. She found her own markets and didn't rely on government-run campaigns for bookings.

I'm overwhelmed trying to keep up with all the marketing demands

There is an inexhaustible obsession with new, Instagrammable tourism experiences and interiors. It is not you; it is the relentless cycle of the marketing industry. Take a deep breath before you react to the incitement to be the best, the biggest, the most, the Superhost, the Tourism Award winner... these programs and status bring exposure benefits, but are not essential for success.

Tourism marketing bodies typically need new and impressive things to market, and the reality is your small venture may not be one. It may be, but you can only launch a new business or product once and ride the wave for a short time before the next thing comes along. You can be under the radar, and very successful in a niche if you are consistent and build your market over time. Ride your own wave.

The government should be helping me more

We are very fortunate in Australia that various levels of government do provide several platforms and support for the industry to work collectively. However, it is really very tiring, and can be a relief when you stop trying to get the government to support you. The fact is, they can't really; they're not geared for it, don't know much about small businesses and probably less about regions and, more specifically, it's out of their remit to be seen to help or favour individual businesses (although it does happen). This area – chasing help and feeling disappointed – is where many new tourism entrepreneurs lose a lot of time and energy –

the false expectations of what help is actually available to them.

The truth is, successful tourism businesses don't need the government as much as the government needs them – a successful regional tourism business. Government needs a healthy vibrant industry for featuring in campaigns, for tax dollars, for jobs, and for the tourism visitor results they often take the credit for. Yes, you need to work with the government. Certainly you must obey the law, but, while government support is nice to have, starting out, it's not essential for success.

So if you want to start a successful, independent regional tourism business, if you have an idea, this book is for you.

If not you, then who? If not now, then when?

YOUR FIRST STEPS

The first steps in starting a new tourism venture are the hardest, because chances are you will be doing it on your own. You may be new to the region, and likely the industry. People in the available support networks such as state tourism bodies, regional tourism organizations and Tourism Industry Councils tend to leave you to it until you can, ironically, demonstrate a level of success and emerge intact with your venture operating - and a few bruises.

Assess your risk appetite

This means you really need to start getting bookings as soon as possible, and build up confidence, whether you are a tour operator, accommodation or an attraction. But before you commit to a tourism venture, and a location, find out the risks and decide what you are prepared to lose, and how you will manage this. It may be $5,000, or $10,000, or nothing at all. Know your risk profile and set a budget.

Do your research

Where you physically start your tourism business will have a massive impact on your success. Ideally, you want to base yourself in an emerging destination where there is untapped growth potential so you can capitalise on future interest. How do you know this? Start to research, and learn the strengths and weaknesses of the destination you are operating in. Normally a good place has a visual appeal, a vibe or a natural aspect, some attractions or activities nearby, and a range of accommodation, but there may be a few market gaps you can fill. Places within an hour or so of a major service centre - but not always - and a place with eating out options. You also need a skilled population of working age so you can employ people and purchase goods and services. See more in Chapter 6 Destinations, Products and Experiences.

Tip: Starting a tourism business in an established community will give you a head start. Tourism works better in established towns where community needs are met, and the town is functioning with power, water, a supermarket, employment, medical services, adequate housing, fuel, and law and order.

Know what things cost

To be a successful operator, you want to earn enough money to pay bills and make decent profits after all expenses are paid. You need to manage the heck out of expenses and keep them down in the first two or three years, and build this as an ongoing habit to grow profits sooner and afford to pay yourself, pay down debt, or invest elsewhere.

No one really enjoys budgeting, do they? So it helps to find your why, and identify your purpose for being in tourism. It may be to pay for your kid's school fees, to even out the farm's cash flow, because it's preferable to host to being a landlord, or because someone in your family desperately needs a career change or fresh start. Whatever it is, knowing your why will help you in times of doubt. But you still need to keep track of costs, to make sure you can pay for that why.

Find a mentor, coach or adviser

Early on, you may face some resistance: this may be your own internal voices, or clearer expressions of disbelief from colleagues, parents, siblings, your children, spouse or friends. You will face early tests and challenges as you heed the call and commit to your new direction, and many people find a mentor or guide helpful at this stage to show them why this path can work for them and what it takes.

If you are in a region far from tourism industry networks or a qualified business mentor, this book will be your guide. Use it to support you as you cross over the threshold from simply being a hobbyist or 'just' a home-based business to becoming a successful regional tourism operator. It requires a different mindset, a new level of commitment, and a willingness to respond to insights to get more bookings and to transition.

By the time you are eligible for tourism support through government programs, you will be seasoned and exhausted, but hopefully clearer about what it is you are selling, and to whom, at what price, and how you can sustain this to make profits and pay yourself enough to make it worth going on. Clearing hurdles is normal and intentional, as that gets you ready for the bigger challenges to come. Getting this far is a milestone that you should celebrate - when you finally muster the energy to peel yourself off the couch!

Register your business

Getting set up with a legal structure takes from one to three months. The basic steps to starting a business in Australia are:

Decide on your business structure

Sole traders and companies are the two most common structures. Sole traders are the simplest and cheapest type of micro or small business, and you can always set up a company later. That costs around $1,200 plus extra accounting fees each year. Plus, companies pay around 26% on profit earned, so sole trader is the best option for starting out small as there is a tax-free threshold on the first $18,000 you earn. There are pros and cons of both options, depending on your end-game. So it helps to think it through. Where do you see yourself in ten years? A company structure will help protect personal assets like your mortgage and other investments should you be sued, or go bankrupt. Noone likes to talk about it, but it happens, especially to businesses not set up or managed properly and especially in volatile markets, which tourism is. If you run an accommodation check with your accountant on the current rules for investment properties and negative gearing, you'll need to decide at a certain occupancy point whether you are a landlord or a business owner for tax and insurance purposes. You can also own a property through your self-managed super fund (SMSF) or through a trust, like a family trust for example, where your kids may be beneficiaries of profits. Discuss your options with your accountant, and make sure that your income and expenses are transparent and easy to track so that you can manage costs as you set up and implement growth plans - to see when you can afford what.

Choose a business name

It's difficult and expensive to change a business name once you have started marketing. Before you fall in love with a name, think it through. Bear in mind that if you plan to sell your business eventually you should not use your own name. For example it would be annoying to buy David Leader's Gippsland Safaris, you'd have to change the name and potentially lose market recognition. Your business name should be something memorable, easy to pronounce, spell and therefore recall and rank in Google searches. The aim of marketing is to reduce barriers to being found by customers, and not be confused with another business with a similar name or product. Do some research on your preferred names on Google to see what other businesses appear. Be prepared to adjust your name so you can stand out. You can do this as a trading name, which is how you are known in the marketplace. It may be the same as your business name, or it may be different. For example, my official business name is Flinders Ranges Outback Shack because Outback Shack was already taken, but I trade legitimately as The Outback Shack. When you are looking for your official business name, research what's available at the Australian Securities Investment Corporation (ASIC). Then consider what you want to trade as, and make sure you add this to the 'Trading As' fields online wherever you can to clear up any confusion behind the scenes in case someone challenges you for stealing intellectual property or their business name.

While it's noble to incorporate non-English or Indigenous naming conventions, research by Indigenous Business Australia shows that when consumers search for Indigenous named tourism companies they don't recall the name correctly, or misspell it, and eventually give up or book something else. It doesn't mean don't use your traditional language, but it is a hard lesson between being politically correct, or even just authentic, and being found and booked sooner. In a mass consumer market, being found, recalled, and remembered is vital, whatever you decide to call yourself. A good search engine optimization strategy can overcome this barrier.

Tip: Keep in mind who your customer is and the language or terminology they are most likely to recall in Google searches if you want to be found. Your business name should also be available as a domain name for web and email addresses.

While you are considering names, check whether the domain is available) so you can secure it, and that there is consistency between your business name, website address, and email address for future marketing.

Get an Australian Business Number (ABN)

Now you have your name and structure sorted, it's time to get your ABN. ABNs are a free and mandatory 11-digit number that identifies your business as legitimate to the Australian community and government, especially for tax purposes. You can register your business name online at the Australian Business Registrar (Applying for an ABN | ABR). Then you can manage your GST status, contact details, and trading names in the ASIC portal. This is where you pay for your business name registration every couple of years. Many small businesses forget or don't know about this ongoing requirement, and can lose the right to their business name, and then their branding rights to their website URL as well if this is challenged. (Note - You don't need to register your brand as Intellectual Property, but you do need to be registered and paid up to be a legitimate business in the eyes of government and the law.)

Register your business name and ABN with your state Department of Business

You will get a certificate indicating you are registered, which you can frame and put on your wall, and pat yourself on the back. At this stage you may be asked to register for GST. You can change this status later, when you earn over $75,000 from business revenue. Otherwise select GST exempt for now. You can also register for an ABN at Business Registration Service if you haven't already done so.

Secure a URL using your business name

The convention in Australia is to have a website URL ending in .com or com.au, however it depends on how and where you build your site. If you create your own site, you can usually purchase a domain within a software program like Squarespace or Wix, and your URL may end in .net or .com. Alternatively, if you just want to secure a domain name aligned to your business name without building a site yet, you can buy a domain outright (or Domain Name System, DNS) from places like Crazy Domains, Go Daddy, Blue Host or HostPapa, and manage your own details. Make sure you have proper anti-virus software installed on your website, and if you do any ecommerce you need a secure server licence (SSL) attached to your host. I recommend this even though it may be a little technically challenging, as it means you retain control of your digital business assets. You can expect to pay around $150 every couple of years to your DNS provider to retain your rights to your domain name, which is now part of your intellectual and brand property.

> **Tip:** Your website is a business asset. Get peace of mind by securing a domain name (DNS) early on and independently of a website designer so you retain control of it throughout the life of your business as you will probably change web designers at some stage, and it will be easier if you have the DNS details at hand. Also, you can learn how to set up new email addresses on the DNS portal, and it's often more cost effective to self-manage.

Tourism terminology

One of the first things people say when they come across the tourism industry is 'All those acronyms!' And you've already seen a few so far. There is definitely a language in tourism, so be ready for it. One of the aims of this book is to familiarise you with tourism terms, acronyms and ecosystems. There is a list of acronyms in the back of the book for quick reference in case you forget, as I will be using them from now on.

What will you learn in this book? How about the FITs - some of whom are also VFRs. New tourism operators can really push your products by working closely with your STO, or with TA if you want to scale to inbound markets early using OTAs. You can also contract ITOs to help you attract internationals, or HVTs, but in the beginning there is some great help from RTOs or RTAs, some of which are funded by LGAs and also RDAs in each region. You can also call on TiCs for accreditation and awards information.

Welcome to Planet Tourism! Here's the decoded version of that paragraph:

What will you learn in this book? How about the free independent travellers - some of whom are also visiting friends and relatives. New tourism operators can really push your products by working closely with your Tourism Commission, or with Tourism Australia if you want to scale to inbound markets early using online travel agents. You can also contract inbound tour operators to help you attract internationals and high-value travellers, but in the beginning there is some great help from regional tourism organisations or regional tourism associations, some of which are funded by local government associations and also Regional Development Australia in each region. You can also call on Tourism Industry Councils for accreditation and awards information.

There. Not so hard. You'll be talking like an industry expert in no time!

Let's summarise

- You can be very successful and make profits in a small or micro business
- Sole trader is a simple business structure, perfect for micro and small businesses
- Register your business name, domain names, and manage your business details regularly to maintain legitimacy
- Research your region's visitor profile, and understand the strengths and weaknesses of your regional destination before you commit
- Know your risk profile - how much money are you prepared to lose?
- Set up in an established town with a functional community if you can
- Choose a business name that's easy for your customers to remember
- The tourism industry's terminology and acronyms are outlined in the Resources section at the end of the book

Mt William (Dulwil), Visit Victoria

CHAPTER TWO

EXPLORING EXPECTATIONS

Let's Get Real

Perhaps you are wondering how to actually do it? After registering a business, what comes next?

Remember, this is not a step-by-step guide. Why? Because I don't believe that approach is realistic. Every business is different, and so it's not a painting by numbers exercise. Although checklists are comforting, and give you direction in a tough patch, your growth into a tourism operator is as individual as you are. I believe building a business is a creative not a linear process. Learning to be patient, and comfortable with ambiguous situations, will help you, as will being on the lookout for how to solve problems as effectively and cheaply as possible. Sometimes you will have to tackle problems more than once before you overcome them. Like any process where you are creating from scratch, bringing something into existence can seem daunting. Your early expectations and the voices in your head may not be helping at this point.

Let's explore some of the common expectations people have about tourism businesses, and look at what often happens and what really matters.

What is running a regional tourism business really like?

You may think running a regional tourism business is fun, a hobby, that you just pursue on weekends and in the school holidays. If you are serious about starting a tourism business and making profits though, not just 'some money', then in most cases these expectations are not realistic.

Here are four common misconceptions about establishing and operating a regional tourism business:

1. We can use the property ourselves and then just rent it out the rest of the time

This one is my favourite – the new Airbnb owner. Your business will eventually need your time, investment and commitment to return income consistently. This is normally what happens:

You start saying to mates at a BBQ "When we aren't using it we have it on Airbnb", and that is true - at first.

You get a few sniffs and low ratings because you are not open when the market wants it, and the house is set up with your grandad's furniture and not the funky kind.

Then you get enquiries for next year, when you haven't even thought about your own family plans yet.

And then the market demand increases in the season when you want to be there yourself, so you can't make the money when you think. Maybe you realise you don't actually get to the holiday house all that often. Your kids want to holiday somewhere else. You now have a second mortgage and another lot of bills and rates, and a mortgage to pay. Your discretionary income is lower, and maybe the economy is taking a turn. Your retirement fund is low.

Your relatives say they'll visit, but don't want to pay you, because, well, they're family.

Enquiries come in, and people ask for a discount because they called direct, and that's what some hotels do, don't they?

You start feeling the pinch and the pressure. No one wants to pay and your tyres are getting kicked. This hobby sucks!

You buy this book.

Congratulations, you have overcome the first expectation and myth of being in tourism. It is not a holiday! But when you start making real money from it, you can certainly fund your next holiday somewhere else.

2. There are plenty of grants out there to pay for our ideas

Grants are plentiful from the government, and also from not for profit organizations and private givers, such as philanthropic foundations and trusts. They often seem more attractive than they are - the devil is in the detail. If you are not established with at least a brand, an ABN and 12 months of trading income, you have little chance of a look-in.

As with any serious capital fundraising, you really need a business plan to show how the idea stacks up, and a return on investment to stakeholders. Otherwise it can come across as an amateur cash grab. Be smart about where you spend your time and energy. Grants are fiercely competitive - consider the opportunity cost of applying for one: can you use your time better elsewhere and leverage the things that are within your control? If there's a small total pool of funds, a short timeframe to respond, only a small grant going per project, and the application process is detailed – beware!

Grants often require a contribution of up to 50%. You are required to pay tax on grants as income. The work to apply for and spend grants is often more than the grant is actually worth. Sometimes you have to wait six months for a decision, when goal posts can change, and deadlines may be extended, giving others an unfair advantage. Then if you win, you have to acquit funds which can be onerous. The thing about free money is it's a myth. Grants can be great, but the best way to invest in your business is to make money, real money by getting more bookings. More about grants under Chapter 7 Regional Characteristics.

There's a Grant Checklist on my website at Clear Vision Consulting under the Resources section. Use it to determine your likelihood of success before you consider any grant as the best way to fund your idea.

3. It's just a bit of fun, how hard can it be

For naturals and extroverts, this is true - they make it look like fun. And some people do make it look easy – perhaps for them it is. Good for them. But if you run a remote business without staff, or live out of the region and have others manage it for you during the year, then you need to think through how you are going to make things work.

Starting and running a small business can be exhausting, terrifying - and exciting. Your head won't shut down, and your body will ache as you put in time at meetings, do the painting and renovating, make the calls, navigate ambiguity, battle with designers to get the website live so you can secure bookings and start to break even. You have a long to-do list of things that you are paying for, and you haven't made a cent yet. So stress can start early.

If you are 100% invested, suddenly you understand what it means to be without a safety net of regular income. You will feel a secret thrill that you are putting yourself out there, and may wonder if anybody actually wants what you have to offer - will they visit, stay, book? And when they do, it feels great when that money lands in your account! If you are running a tourism business as more than a hobby, learning new skills takes time, even if you desperately need to succeed. Self-management techniques can help with the stress.

When moving from a hobby to a business, it's important to be patient and work through challenges. Realistically, it takes 12- 24 months to start getting bookings and see a pattern emerge through holidays and the seasons as you grow. This book will help you to focus on what matters most from the customer's point of view, and how to get the bookings and keep getting them.

4. I'm gonna make a motza, maaaaaate

I really hope you do! But the statistics show otherwise. Tourism businesses are mostly small operations. The number of micro businesses has grown by 10%, from 1.4 million in June 2021 to 1.5 million in June 2022. That's 100,000 new SMEs in one year. At June 2021:

45% | **Almost half (45%) of tourism businesses had no employees other than the owner**

33% | **33% had between one and four employees**

The ABS definition of a small business is one that has 19 or less employees and makes under $10 million a year. If you are making $10m a year, you are by most ordinary peoples' definition, not small!

Most of the tourism sector in Australia has a very low turnover - under $50,000. Average business turnover in 2021 was lower than in 2016. This is due to a greater share of businesses with turnover of less than $50k in the visitor economy. Most are micro sole operator businesses, and many have other incomes supporting their enterprise, or are running the business from superannuation or other reserves.

At June 2021, over half of all tourism businesses in Australia (53%) had annual revenues of less than $200,000. Only 10% had revenues of more than $2 million a year, and 47% of regional businesses had revenues of less than $200,000 a year.

During COVID, many businesses survived thanks to government support for workers' wages, and only now are we seeing the impact since subsidies have been withdrawn. But small business owners' pockets are not deep, and many marginal tourism operators are at a high risk of leaving the industry. If you can scale and find the workforce, and survive the many external issues impacting the industry, global crisis, recession, GFC, pandemic, you are extremely fortunate or doing very well.

But using some of the strategies and frameworks I suggest in this book can forewarn and forearm you so you are ready to deal with the challenges of being small, remote and working as a family to help visitors to explore this amazing country we get to call home.

Shit happens - all the time

Tourism is beset by external forces like no other industry – pilots strike, pandemics, climate change and freak weather, interest rate rises, mining growth, school closures, event closures, roads washed out, global economic meltdowns, wars, rising fuel prices... These external forces may or may not impact you as regions have different economies to cities, and as COVID showed us, some regions thrived during global economic contraction, while other regions and many cities fell silent.

Large global or national economic shocks like recessions, higher interest rates, and pandemics affect the money left in people's pockets to take holidays, and the number of people willing or able to physically get to your regional destination. You will need to keep on your toes, and persuade other businesses to join forces and create a collective approach if you want to survive in regional tourism.

Knowing your regional cycle can help you prepare for tough times. Your regional cycle is characterised by the industries operating there, the population features, and weather patterns shaping seasonality. On a big picture level, tourism is an industry that reinvents itself often - after 10 years you will see a cycle where small businesses grow and are bought out by larger businesses, who consolidate and restructure. After large economic events like recessions, smaller businesses without scale or reserves opt out and close or are bought out by bigger ones. This may also be part of your endgame plan, as we cover in Chapter 5 Welcome to Planet Tourism.

Tip: There are few tourism businesses listed on the ASX, which tells you something about the the volume of SMEs that constitute the industry and the volatility of the marketplace we are in.

What good looks like - regions where tourism works

Have you ever said "Wow, this place is awesome. I'm having such a good time, people are great, the service is friendly, and everything's just falling into place. This place rocks!" This is no coincidence. You know you are in an established region when operators work well together. It's a sign that the local operators have collaborated, and staff are not just staff, but are invested in the business purpose, in the community or town, and are happy to share local knowledge and support each other. In remote regions, the only way to survive is together, paying it forward and across, referring guests to restaurants, accommodation, and attractions - cross-selling at each other's receptions: "Sorry, I'm booked out, but I'll call ahead and find you another room." No fear of competition. It's a shared understanding that visitors are good for the town, and everybody benefits from tourism spend, from the service station to the supermarket, to the year 10 student working in the kitchen, to the mechanic fixing the tour bus. In most regions, you have a limited season to make money, and when there's plenty, it helps to share it around. This happens naturally when people are passionate about their place, and have been through ups and downs. Regions which have experienced tough times in tourism don't take success for granted.

Case Study 1

A change in access can make or break a region Alice Springs, NT

In the early 2000s, there were frequent direct flights from Sydney, Melbourne and Adelaide to Alice Springs. Tourists then went by road or took a separate flight to Yulara, the iconic outback town four and a half hours away at the base of the real drawcard, Uluru-Kata Tjuta National Park. Alice Springs was booming with tours, casinos, art galleries, charter buses, hotels and restaurants filled with visitors from all over the world enthralled by the magnificent desert. Then flights went direct to Yulara and half of the market chose to fly direct, almost crippling Alice where the majority of the population lived. Operators rallied to save their businesses. They did better destination marketing, selling the region around Alice Springs, found new markets, trained agents on the benefits of selling Alice Springs, lobbied the government to subsidise seats and see public servants flew Jetstar and not just Qantas to keep a budget airline active so backpackers would keep coming and ensure volume not just yield. Industry looked after bread-and-butter markets like the self-drive markets, and worked harder to give those who did fly into Alice great experiences of lesser-known neighbouring places.

"It's not you, it's the economy, stupid!"

Ex-Federal Treasurer Paul Keating was not only hilarious, but also on the money with this often-quoted phrase. As you will see in Chapter 5, some things are in your control and others are not. The economy is in the latter category. And the economy is beset by the many ups and downs that create the market conditions for your business and your customers. Are people confident and spending? Are they tightening their purse strings? Is inflation biting, or are interest rates headed down? You may find yourself in a region with a tourism industry that is new, inexperienced, or established but with its head stuck in the sand – or, hopefully, one that has been down this road before, and where operators, Council and community are able to respond flexibly to economic conditions together and in a timely way. Regions have different economic drivers, because demand for services and goods is higher than in cities, due to lack of local options and suppliers, and the local industries are different: agriculture, energy, primary production, trades. Finally, transport, roads and air access vary from region to region, which plays a huge role in who comes and goes, and how frequently, the shape of the tourism industry, and how visitors move and buy in a region.

Case Study 2

Don't know what you've got till it's gone Southwest WA

In 2018, Western Australia was enjoying high levels of employment, a strong mining sector, and infrastructure that always seemed to me to have a kind of gleam from generous tax spending. Employment was high, wage growth was strong, people drove new cars. Boom time. All the time. Right?

Wrong. Well, mostly.

WA's economy is strongly linked to China's, and when China's building boom slowed and iron ore prices dropped, WA jobs were lost, house prices fell, and there was less money to spend. The impact tore through to regional tourism. Suddenly intrastate visitors (that's locals) weren't spending as much on travel. They started to save their cash, or prioritised interstate or overseas holidays that were better value for money. Tourism operators had got used to good times being normal. Many hadn't bothered to invest in marketing for 10 years; they simply captured the local market as wealthy people drove by. Suddenly, regional tourism operators were unable to pay their bills. Marriages faltered and debts grew. Business owners were in real distress. Many operators did not know how to ask for help, or where to go to get it. And government help was not readily available. People were caught flat-footed.

A local consulting company in Bunbury contracted me to work with the tourism industry, and apply the strategies I outline in this book:

- Making it easier for people to book and buy, keeping them lingering and spending more
- Creating experiences and services, delivering them in new ways, and taking risks
- Talking to councils about building trails through the forests to give people more to do, and more reasons to visit and stay longer
- Getting the industry to work together, refer business and cross-promote

Many in the industry had forgotten how to work together. They were all out of practice – they'd had no need. But when it matters, and even when it doesn't, successful regional tourism operators come together to problem solve, to share ideas, and to try new things.

This is what good looks like. These are industry and destination level strategies for you to keep in mind as you build your business, which are covered in more detail in the next chapters.

Network or die

Sound a bit dramatic? Your network is a life support system unique to you that helps you deal with difficult times. When you are committed in your tourism business, and when shit happens as it always does, you need to be able to respond. You need a constant supply of bookings, bookings, and more bookings. Referrals and real opportunities are what matter. Not more talk. Unless it leads to bookings. Not a social media plan. Not branding. But actual bookings, and these can come from within your network. Learning how to network is free, and a skill you can develop by watching, and practising online tutorials.

Your personal and professional network is the single most important thing within your power that can help you drive referrals after your distribution systems.

This is why I recommend joining a professional networking group with a shared purpose, such as your Regional Tourism Organisation (RTO), Tourism Industry Councils (TiCs) or groups like Business Network International.

Why BNI? It's great to work within your industry, but I've often found it's equally beneficial to be the odd one out from time to time. BNI selects members in each chapter, based on your sector; they foster a non-competitive membership, and their mission is to refer business to one another, and keep track of the value they create collectively. Your network is a secret weapon in a seasonal industry as every bit helps. When things get bad, you have no time to waste. You'll need to fire up your networks and get bookings somehow, and it's usually working with others who are invested, engaged, motivated and accountable.

Sometimes I get asked about Chambers of Commerce - whether to join one. Chambers are as good as the people running them, and the energy of their members. Some thrive in regions like in the Northern Territory where members meet, network proactively, and the business community is small but connected. Everyone knows everyone in a small pond, and you can get to know other large business owners quickly and well in a regional context. People build relationships and win work there. In other regions, Chambers may be a bit old-fashioned, and there are more modern networking groups and referral options to be found on Facebook groups. Ask any Gen Y or Gen X in your life, are they or do they know anyone who is a member of a Chamber of Commerce? If they look at you blankly then you have your answer. Chambers are great if you want training and employment advice, and access to a broad church of industries and businesses. You might stand out as the only tourism operator, or get a booking for a network colleague who has family coming to town, or find your new bookkeeper at an event. It does help to have a profile later on in your business journey in an extended group. If you are considering joining a Chamber, ask if you can attend a function first to see if it's your style before committing to fees, and ask for their forward schedule of events and guest speakers to see if they are progressive, talking about issues that affect small tourism businesses today, or just dusting off old playbooks.

THE HARD LESSONS

Be clear about your purpose

I encourage you to understand what is motivating you to go into tourism. You don't need to have a great social cause, because it's perfectly fine to just make money. Being clear about your 'why' will help when you need to recommit to the business. It removes the emotion, so that you can just get on with doing what needs doing, and troubleshoot when things get rocky. You will come back to your 'why' often as you double down to keep focused.

You will need to tap into your motivation to channel energy to renovate, rebrand, stay positive, and build your capacity if you are doing something new and hard, like scaling to service more bookings and more demand. Capacity can increase with more resources and energy - and not just your own. You can increase capacity by buying in help, paying a friend or family member, employing a work experience student. Know how much you are willing to invest or - another way of looking at it - how much you can afford to lose.

Know your values

Your values and boundaries will help your business to attract the kind of visitors you want, and not get stuck with people who waste time expecting you to chase them, or demanding refunds because they didn't read the instructions you sent. Sometimes you get burnt, but it's ok, that happens to everybody. But let it happen a second or third time, and that's on you.

Being clear (and kind) upfront will minimise any misunderstandings and unrealistic expectations from your guests, and save you a lot of trouble down the track. There are many ways to say no gently without being rude, and most people appreciate it.

Manage your emotions

Tourism is very much a people industry. People have strong feelings about what they expect and what they're entitled to, who you are, and what the contract is. Wherever there is money there is emotion. Some guests treat tourism operators like they are negotiating a deal of a lifetime, or auctioning a house, pitting you against your competitor to get the best deal. Personally, I have no time for this. I am not a haggler, and tend to increase my prices whenever I'm being hassled by someone who won't just pay the price but wants to take my time too. If you get involved in horse-trading or constant bargaining, you can get emotionally involved and quickly waste energy over things of small value in the scheme of things - and may miss the bigger opportunities when they surface.

Emotions and money both come and go. Money is what others give you for the value you are promising to give in return. The emotion is in the expectation and the delivery, so if they fall short, there's disappointment. To manage time and avoid the potential for conflict, it helps to put things in writing, especially for accommodation and tour bookings. State your offer, inclusions and exclusions upfront, make options clear, and negotiate the rest later if you want to.

Managing your emotions and your time will put you on the front foot so you are not caught off-guard when someone surprises you with rudeness, criticism or overstepping the mark. All you can do is provide clear information and guidelines and reinforce them, leaving people to choose your business or not.

You are not your business - but you are responsible for it

Australian entrepreneur Mark Bouris talks about this in his book *What it Takes*. I loved the book - Mark just calls it like it is. I've had a few epiphanies listening to him, and his podcast too. The big one was needing to separate my personal feelings and identity to try and fix things, to be able to cut my losses and move on. It was a bit clunky, but also the start of a new way of operating for me.

When you start out, your business is like a baby - it needs your time and attention. It can feel like a part of you, and it's a great feeling - you evolve, it grows, the money comes in, and you think wow! Look at how great I'm doing! You create value that wasn't there before. It's a fantastic feeling. Then something goes wrong and you become unsure, your confidence goes and perhaps you become financially stretched then stressed, caught up in dramas.

If you are responsible for success, then you must also be responsible for failure, right? Well, not exactly. My point is - as Paul Keating reminded us, it could be the economy - perhaps you are not as influential as you thought. It could be the economy, stupid! There are positive and negative forces out of your control; often you are riding a wave, not necessarily responsible for creating it. Overidentifying personally and egotistically with your success in your business - the good and the bad - can put you in the firing line. You need to be able to let go of things and trust in your offer overall for the long term, not just the short term. If you learn to disassociate yourself from the business, it can take shape and grow in response to business needs. You can make tough decisions more readily as it is not about you, but about the circumstances impacting the business. The business is a vehicle to enable you to create value, and charge for it. It is a powerhouse of your own creation, and a very cool thing to witness working. But if it's not working, you need to make tough calls. Your business relies on you, not the other way around.

Stop blaming others and take control

This will only make sense when you've started something new, had some runs on the board, lost staff, or had complaints or an incident where you are being shown things have to change if you want to keep this business going without losing your mind or losing money. Stop blaming others for things that aren't working, and take some time to sit quietly with the problem. Go back to basics and recommit in your own mind to "this is what I want to do and I will do it, and I will do it as well as I can and be happy with that." If you are withholding, skimping, or avoiding your end of the contract, you are damaging your business and ability to make money in future.

If you want to be a successful tourism operator and make money, you must follow through on your end of the deal. It doesn't matter how you feel about it, or what you want to feel about it, or if your customer is not feeling it... or if it's a Sunday and you are out with friends and you get a call because there's no water, or there's a possum going off in a tour bus. If you are in charge and get a message that something's not right, you need to respond and deal with the problem. You are responsible, and the buck stops with you.

Regional Tourism Operation Basics

If you provide the basics really well, you can satisfy 85% of your customers most of the time. People are generally happy, and want to get on with their holiday or reason for being in your region or town. You can compete over time on doing the basics well, consistently and charging a fair price. A booking is a booking, and money is money, so don't overcomplicate it. If you cannot get organic Himalayan Iceberg Tea in your country town, and some magazine is telling you that's what people like, take a deep breath... and trust that a Bushells is enough for most guests.

They are just happy to be on holiday in your region, and not arguing about whose turn it is to wash the dishes. People are prepared to pay you to escape their own lives - this is the big secret!

Now, let's make some money!

Here are some basic operating principles for accommodation, tours and attractions:

Accommodation

This advice is for small accommodation, such as holiday houses, campgrounds, bespoke boutique hotels and the like:

- **A good night's sleep** - Invest in decent mattresses and bedding and towels, and you will lift your reviews into a whole new star rating bracket. If you are in a campsite, make sure the party people are done by 9pm. Campers get up early.
- **Cleanliness** - You will be rated on this, so make sure you train your cleaner how you want it done. No fluff balls or dusty skirting boards. Replace chipped cups. Schedule regular cleans, deep cleans, and external building cleans through the months and seasons.
- **Clear directions** - Get yourself on Google Maps by setting up a Google Business account as soon as possible, and send clear directions and check-in instructions in advance.
- **A decent meal** - If you're not providing meals, tell guests where you like to eat or what's good within a 10-minute drive or walk. Remember, they may be arriving late, so quick and open is the priority, otherwise offer to arrange some supper for them for a fee.
- **Reliable heating and cooling** - Provide the means to get warm: blankets, fans, bar heaters, wood for wood fires. A cold pool, ice, air conditioning or a fan in summer. Just give it to them - don't be stingy.

- **A cup of tea or coffee** - A warm drink is a shared human comfort all over the world. You don't have to go over the top, but it's not a big investment to buy some decent tea and coffee and provide long-life milk and sugar.

- **A place to withdraw local currency** - Australians are among the biggest users of payWave in the world, but your overseas and older visitors may not be. Tell them if they need to bring cash or can withdraw it from a local ATM.

- **Simple instructions** - How to turn on the TV, use the Wi-Fi passcode, operate your cranky stove, access the site in the dark, what to do in an emergency.

Tours

This advice is generally for vehicle based tours but also walking and guided tours by bike or canoe for example.

- **Consistent departure times** - Set departure times and dates consistently so local accommodation and agents can remember when referring people to you. You can always cancel a tour or tailor it, but if you want direct bookings then have availability and departure times on your web calendar. If you want to stand out, be available on public holidays, weekends and at Christmas as this is when visitors are looking for things to do.

- **Be known for something** - Give tours a distinctive name so people can differentiate, and list all inclusions for tours. A core product that everyone knows.

- **Presentation and cleanliness** - Your guides' uniforms and vehicles make the first impression. If your tour guide is barefoot and it's not a surfing or meditation tour, it's sayonara, hippy! Have new, clean vehicles. After each tour, wash the vehicle, and wash the uniform - maintain, organise and update.

- **Branding** - Have cars, uniforms, bikes or buses clearly branded with your logo and name so people know which bus/car/bike to get onto in the carpark.

- **Have essentials on board** - Snacks, water, sunscreen, phone-charging outlets, tissues, first aid kit. Being prepared is a sign of professionalism, and won't have you scrambling when your guests need that one little thing to get comfortable. It's the small things that make a big difference.

- **Safety and communication 24/7** - Have a means to communicate in emergencies at all times and keep your confidence high. Also keep phones charged, spare batteries on board, and a two-way radio or satellite phone if you are going out of range. Test regularly! Invest in an E-PIRB emergency locator beacon for group safety if you are going remote.

- **Manifest and printed itinerary** - You will need to know who is on board at all times, contact details, and a copy of their pickup and drop off locations. Print out the itinerary and laminate it so you can hand it out and save having to repeat yourself. Make sure your guests are on the tour they booked. It sounds basic, but you'd be surprised.

- **Volume** - If you are guiding while driving, don't talk the whole time or play loud music. People need a break so they can just be on the tour with their own thoughts. Choose your times, be empathetic to cultures, age groups, disabilities and demographic preferences.

Attractions

This advice is for attractions with a bricks and mortar experience but can be adapted for other kinds of natural and cultural attractions and activities for food and wine tasting, parks and gardens, events and shopping precincts.

- **Consistent opening hours that work for visitors** - When you chop and change opening hours it creates market confusion, and you invite death by 1,000 cuts. If people arrive and your attraction is closed even though your Google hours say it's open, people rightly get annoyed, rate and review publicly, and rarely return. Serious tourism attractions are open 365 days a year. Not everyone celebrates the same calendar year or religious festivals. We are in a diverse multicultural society, and more and more visitors from non-Anglo-Celtic cultures come to enjoy the Australian lifestyle.

If you are open when other attractions are closed on public holidays, this means an opportunity for you. Visitors from big cities expect to be able to take in cultural activities, even if the hours are limited. If you are closed on a Sunday, you could be missing vital trade. Especially in a food and wine region, where people with young children are looking for things to do apart from eating and drinking.

- **Clear signs you are open** - Invest in professional outdoor banners, flags, sandwich boards on the streets: colourful external signs that you are open for business.

- **A strong entrance experience** - An uncluttered entrance is accessible. It can be well lit (or dark if that's the experience, like a Haunted House) and welcoming (or terrifying). The entrance experience should evoke an emotion and set the tone - whatever it is. Make sure someone meets people at the entrance. Visitors should have good directions for what to do next. If it's a DIY entry, they need to understand this in advance. More on entry and exit experiences under the 5Es later in the book.

- **Good visitor flow** - Design your attraction space so that people move in one direction or have enough room to move around without social awkwardness. Think about visitor flow, and don't forget to use outside spaces too.

- **Orientate with a map** - If your attraction is a garden, an amusement park, or a heritage site over multiple buildings, develop a mud map so people know where to go and what to see, and can arrange their experience according to their preference.

- **Make ticketing and entry prices easy to understand** - Consider how you charge and take payment. Will you charge locals? Encourage people to book online to promote forward bookings and help plan staff rosters and avoid queues? Does entrance include a cup of coffee or an additional value add to share the business around town?

- **Accessible toilets** - Yep, people need them, and need to change babies, a private place to breastfeed or take medication with access for walkers and wheelchairs. Signpost them clearly, and make sure they are clean and stocked throughout the day.

- **Exit experience** - People should finish their experience on a good note. You may direct them to the local coffee shop, another attraction referral, or invite them to look at the merchandise or stay for a glass of wine or a cup of tea before they leave if you are set up to offer it to them.

Let's summarise

- A tourism business will eventually need your time, investment, and commitment to get consistent bookings
- Grants are hard to win as a start-up, but a great way to use someone else's money to invest in a pilot idea
- Regions where tourism works are usually established, pay referrals forward, work together, and are in functional communities where basic needs are covered
- Separate your identity from your business brand to make the hard calls when you need to, take risks, and focus on what matters
- You can compete by consistently doing the basics well
- Attractions rely on reliable opening hours and year-round traffic
- People travel and want places to eat, and things to see and do on weekends and public holidays. Attract multicultural visitors by opening on public holidays and weekends

Silky Oaks Lodge, Tourism and Events Queensland

CHAPTER THREE

Regional Tourism Marketing Essentials

So what does marketing actually mean?

One of the things I often hear is "Yes, I am interested in marketing, but how do I get bookings? How will people find me?" You may struggle to connect with your customers when you can't yet see them, talk to them or know them.

Marketing. It's like golf - the harder you try the more elusive it seems. Only when you stay focused and relax, trust you have done the work, then the bookings come.

So what is marketing? Here's my favourite definition:

"It's being in front of the right people at the right time with a product or service they want at the right price."

See. Just like golf. It sounds so simple - just get the ball in the hole. Marketing, like golf, is made up of many disciplines. The best, and even some of the worst, golfers spend hours perfecting each discipline; driving and putting are the metaphorical equivalents of branding and winning online bookings.

Marketing as a theory is different to the practice. Like most things, the practice is where you get the most benefit, and as a business owner you will be practising and refining for a few years before you perfect your swing. You may find you enjoy or are better at some aspects than others; you may prefer direct customer service over social media.

But being able to master some marketing basics is necessary if you want to be successful in the Australian regional tourism industry.

And this is because more often than not, in regions you are physically a long way from where your largest markets live. So you will rely on marketing to do your heavy lifting for you when you can't be there in person.

The key to successful marketing is to practise across all the disciplines to have a complete understanding of the game. Work out what you absolutely need to start with, what can wait until later, and what you can outsource when you can afford to.

Did you know that across the main golfing skill areas like putting, driving, chipping, Tiger Woods was not number one in any? He was in the top three and that was enough to secure the major golf titles in the world. My point is, you don't have to be the best all the time at everything to win bookings. You don't even need to be in the top ten.

But you do need to make an effort, and show up to skills tutorials to get better and more confident. You can master tourism marketing enough to have a presence, secure bookings, and grow your business. But it won't be a hole in one. You'll need to chip away. Ok, no more golf puns. Promise.

5 Ps of marketing

Marketing theory refers to the four or five Ps of marketing, depending on who's telling the story. These form the framework of my approach to tourism marketing, beyond the heavy focus on promotion, and they are: People, Product, Price, Promotion and Position. This book is focused on all of these, as it takes more than just promotion to attract and grow bookings. Your market and physical position, price, and the quality of the experience you offer are often overlooked as strategies for maximising your income.

1. People

Tourism is all about people. This P refers to your customers. It can also refer to your staff as the face of your business.

What are your customers telling you?

Their feedback?

How do they enquire?

How do they book?

What are their needs?

Use your own experiences as a visitor in your own business, as chances are others have similar frustrations, needs and expectations too. Research Regional Tourism profiles to learn about visitor characteristics in your region (see Resources by Chapter).

2. Product

This is the thing you are selling: the tour, the craft beer, the hire car or the hotel room. The trick with product is that it can be an experience or a service. Products have features, and provide benefits, but knowing the difference is essential when you sell and price the product, and demonstrate value for money.

Your product design should best fit a certain kind of customer. Which would a business traveller choose: a classic, modern hotel room or a treehouse in an old growth forest that you need to hike to?

3. Price

Price reflects value, and is one of the most underestimated Ps of tourism marketing strategy in my view. Another way to think about value is, what is the benefit minus the risk to the customer. If risks are low and benefits are high, the value is high and should cost more. Price is flexible, moveable and normally goes up with increased costs (like inflation, wages or CPI), or if a business starts to compete for a higher-fee-paying client, and if the competition at the middle level is fierce. Consider adding lots of value and charging more in regions as city folk are used to paying more than many regional businesses charge. Price can also be used to launch quickly in the market, and get a brand or new service out there while you develop the next product at a higher price. You can have a range of tours or rooms at different prices for different markets. Prices should cover all the costs to you as an operator, include commission to third parties, and also a healthy profit margin. See more in Chapter 4, Using price strategically over time.

4. Position

This refers to both your geographic position, which can really help with exposure and foot traffic, essential if you are an attraction, and also to your place in the market compared to the competition. Are you low or high priced? Mid-range?

Position and price work together. Are you the first to hit the market with a new tour or idea in your town? First movers have a strong advantage, but watch out. Being new is sometimes risky, and you have to invest to launch and find a new customer base. It is much easier for a second mover to tap into the demand you have created and compete for market share. You might price low to start with, and increase over time to maximise your profit if others take market share using your first mover position.

5. Promotion

This includes all the digital tools such as your website, social media accounts, and content on third party booking sites such as Bookings.com or Hipcamp. It also includes the way you write about your products and experiences, the imagery you use, your colours, brand values and logo. It is the bookings journey your customers go on - how you appear when they are researching the region, and things to do. Are you in the Visitor Guide? Were you at the Caravan Show? Are you on Google Maps and Facebook? Have you been on the radio or in the news lately? Featured in a regional or state campaign? This includes reviews, how others see you, distribution (there's a whole section on this later in this chapter), and managing your public profile as a business.

So that's people, product, price and position in a nutshell.

Key takeaway: the Ps work together, so if your price is too high and your product not quite right, bookings will slow down. If you are flat out and can't keep up, the market is valuing what you do, so consider raising your prices to maximise profit without exhausting your staff. It may be time to expand. If bookings peter out, and you have done everything else, you may need to promote new products pronto.

Tip: Promotions are not the only way to get bookings. Much of the time, if your destination has a strong appeal, you will win business because of the regional profile, and because your product and price are at the right level. But you still need to be found.

STAGES OF A TRAVELLER'S BOOKING LIFE CYCLE

Years ago, some bright spark identified the distinct stages of a traveller's booking life cycle that starts long before purchasing a tour, bed night or hire car. This description is now widely adopted in the travel industry, and you will find versions all over the Internet.

Marketers have been plotting and studying the psychology of our behaviours for years to monetise our habits, create desire and facilitate spending in frictionless ways. It's worth understanding this as you plan your business. If you can see where customers are in the life cycle, you will know how best to respond and more likely secure the booking. Are they browsing and researching, or ready to purchase? Have they just finished a holiday and starting to dream about the next? Recognising this will have you ready to respond when customers enquire, and save you time.

The diagram below illustrates the different stages of a traveller's booking cycle:

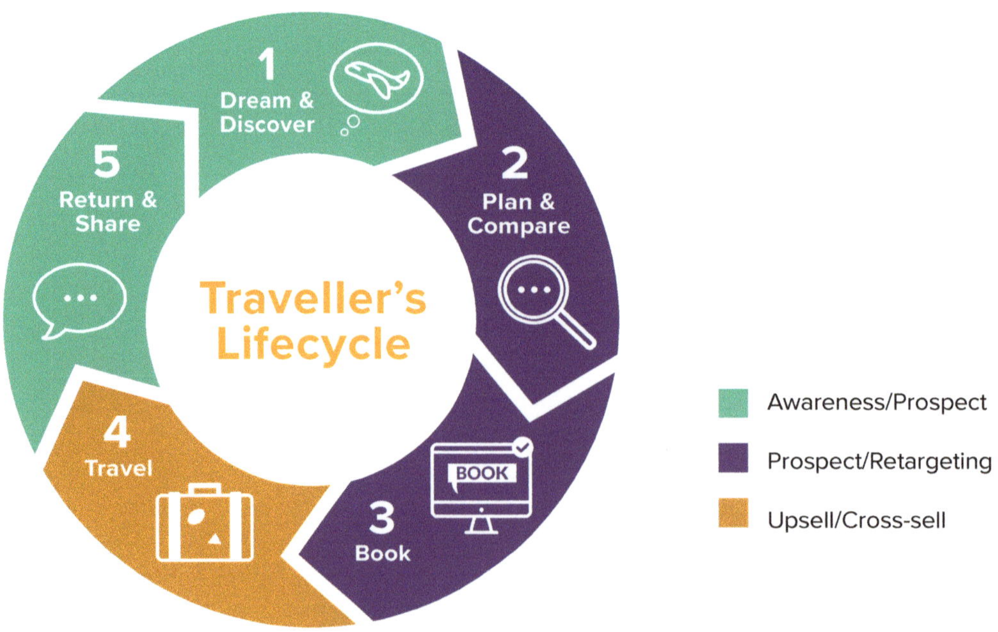

Here are those stages (plus one more) in more detail:

1. Dream and discover

Travellers are researching, talking to friends, and narrowing down options for destinations and experiences. They are on the radar for experiences and places that appeal to core values and the types of experiences they want to have.

2. Plan and compare

Now they are actively searching blogs, websites, destination guides, buying the Lonely Planet, signing up for special flight deals, and researching seasonality and tour or accommodation availability. They are setting dates and budgets, piecing an itinerary together, and really learning about the region or town they will be exploring.

3. Book

Here they are, starting to lay down the cash and commit to a place or a journey. Most people buy the flights or book the hire car, then start to book accommodation; these are generally the two highest value purchases on a holiday. Some will book tours early if this is the deciding factor, for example the multi-night Overland Track hike in Tasmania has a short season with capped daily departures, or a specialist dance school where limited enrolments have opened for students to train with a renowned teacher. These get booked first, and then flights and accommodation follow.

4. Anticipate

I added this one as it's often overlooked: the holiday vibes are born and creeping into the everyday. Now that travellers are committed, excitement builds as they look forward to the trip. They start to share with friends and social networks, are alert to news from that region, receptive to extra information needed before their arrival such as weather warnings, check-in information and 'don't forget to pack' tips. This is a good time to upsell and cross sell if you haven't sent options to them already, as people spend more in anticipation phases.

5. Travel

Visitors are at their destination, and experiencing the region, the service, and the tours and food on offer. They are taking photos, sharing on social media, reviewing and rating places on Google Review. They may be booking new tours and accommodation in the region.

6. Return and share

As visitors leave a place, they start to reflect and compare their experience with their expectations and make judgements. Was it more or less than they expected? They may compare notes with other travellers, share and rate on social media, Trip Advisor, the Airbnb ratings apps. They distribute the merch and souvenirs they wouldn't buy anywhere else to people when they get home as a way of sharing the adventure.

Using this diagram and the stages, you can correlate the tools, media, and information visitors need and look for at different stages, and how this relates to you having a presence on social media, Facebook, Instagram or TikTok, depending on your target market and where they get their information. These days, it's hard to deny the accessibility and ease of sharing on social media and the power of websites or Google Maps - links are easy to capture and share on the move at the touch of a few buttons, so decisions can be made much faster, and you benefit if you are easy to find. More on social media under Chapter 4 Marketing on a budget.

WHO ARE YOUR MARKETS?

If you've been on the ground watching the cars full of sticky-fingered children circle the block looking for the entrance to the Whale Centre, or been behind the 4WDs covered in stickers from The Best Bakehouse at the Back of Wahoo, then you are among independent self-drivers. If you've fielded enquiries (or perhaps asked any of the following yourself) about where to eat late with kids, if a hotel has a no-step shower and wheelchair access, how to fix a broken axle, or book such and such tour, then you may already know the special needs and queries of the self-drive market.

Self-drivers

Self-drivers are common in regions, yet often overlooked for more glamorous market segments, particularly higher-yielding markets that fly or are hosted in private vehicles. Pre-organised and pre-booked tours and flight itineraries are easier to track and measure in research data, so perhaps that gives these segments a higher profile. But I firmly believe the self-drive market is a powerhouse, and this is understood by caravan park investors, supermarkets like Coles and Woolworths, and petrol stations along Australia's regional highways.

Regions outside of lush farming communities or hotspots with good aeroplane or cruise ship access, will generally rely on a domestic self-drive market. So getting to know your bread and butter - and which side of the bread is buttered - will help you to develop products and experiences, get good reviews, meet needs, and win more bookings.

In most regions without airline access, there are three main markets - particularly caravanners and 4WDers - you will get to know, which provide bread and butter cashflow, and are often viewed as one homogenous group. But there are distinct segments, each with different preferences, needs and interests, and they travel different routes. State tourism marketing people will mention them in passing, but at the coalface these markets will come into vivid focus for you as you begin to respond to their unexpected questions, take bookings, meet them at the door, and clean up after them, day in and day out. They are:

- **Families or couples in conventional cars**

  Travelling in the school holidays mostly, but also for regional sports, and visiting friends and relatives (the VFR market) for parties, funerals, anniversaries. Interested in cabins, quirky or romantic BnBs, or farm stays if they live in cities and farms are a novelty. Many families will also car camp with conventional vehicles and stay on farms and in National Parks.

- **Caravanners**

  Young families and older couples. The older couples have time for long-haul trips, and many do short breaks to visit family or bucket list destinations. They stay in caravan parks mostly, but occasionally in a holiday home to repair vehicles or for a break.

This market is often characterised by a partner who doesn't want to rough it, and the other who is done with the back breaking work of hoisting pop-up trailers, or erecting tents in the dark. More time for four o'clock wine!

- **Four-wheel drivers**

  Middle-aged couples, young families and the blokes. They can tow camper trailers as a family unit, or be part of a club and travel in convoys. They are self-contained and independent with their own camping gear, and stay in caravan parks, National Parks or farm stays with campsites and long drop toilets.

- **International self-drivers**

  These days free independent travellers (FITs) such as backpackers are relatively wealthy, sometimes travelling in their middle years (40-60), hiring cars and campervans, and driving long-haul across Australia with all the other campers and caravanners. This market is a real shapeshifter, hard to track and research, and a large percentage is from overseas. Some may live temporarily in Australia on work or student visas and be traveling with visiting family. The FITs are very valuable to the economy because they are real experience seekers, not pampered travellers. They travel far and wide, and will pay for authentic experiences in regions that offer simple Australian nature-based soft adventures - camping, hiking, bike-packing, 4WDing, night picnics, shearing demonstrations, campfire cooking classes, outdoor painting classes, wellness retreats, Indigenous experiences, overnight sailing adventures, treehouse lodging, for example. Research shows that long-haulers budget on accommodation as they spend many nights on the road, but value experiences, and willingly pay more for memory-making adventures, food and gifts.

Markets within markets

You may hear the self-drive market called unstructured, meaning people book experiences and accommodation independently, often at the very last minute. This is an increasing phenomenon as more options are available. Unstructured sometimes feels hard to track, but over time you will learn your customers' habits: the time they arrive, questions they ask, what draws them in, and what they comment on.

Here are seven self-drive market segments you will encounter:

1. Grey nomads

Grey nomads are a generation of savers: they love 'free', and may free camp in highway rest areas and reserves on long-haul holidays to save money. And they love museums and attractions, stay in caravan parks and self-cater - and they shop for souvenirs.

2. Families bush camping and 4WDers

Technically two segments, but they may be the same. Families in vans and campers may be attracted to theme parks, native gardens and local galleries - bakeries definitely. This group may need a couple of nights in a small hotel or B&B to wash clothes, fix the rig, stock up, and send some emails before heading off on the next leg.

Bush 4WDers are a funny lot. They often seem to care more about their gear and gadgets than the environment they travel so far for, and while they love driving in nature they are not keen on actually walking around or taking exercise. They prefer their cars to do the work, climbing the impossible and getting off the beaten track. They prefer to drive on beaches and watch from the windows. Some are solo, some travel in convoy, but this crowd is equipped to survive doomsday. They are DIY self-catering all the way, stopping at pubs, bakeries, to discuss new tracks with fellow travellers or maybe stop at the mechanic. They want cheap/free secret camp spots, ironically preferring places where there are no cars.

3. Visiting friends and relatives (VFR)

VFRs are an excellent market as they rely on locals to refer them and are generally interested in seeing family, eating out, and a day trip to the must-do/see attractions. They are a year-round market, travel for all occasions, happy or sad, and may know the region already if they are a repeat market.

4. Bushwalkers and mountain bikers

This crowd uses their legs and are great at interacting with the community, because they are on foot and seek out nature and wilderness. They want networks of trails, and directional links to cafés, pubs and towns, transfers and a place to wash bikes, store gear safely and sleep well. They are self-catering and low impact, great for small towns, close to nature, and like places with small populations.

5. Business travellers

Business customers want great Wi-Fi (doesn't everyone?), a good night's sleep, and the best breakfast and coffee they can get their hands on at 7am. Even better if they can swim or run somewhere if they are that way inclined, and like to keep up routines on the road. They often leave early. A low fuss, often repeat market, they travel year-round and are happy to spend a bit more as it's often not their money paying the account.

6. Short stay couples

Couples want a weekend away, some things of interest to do, and low fuss. Often they are working age with no kids, and happy to travel light and explore your town. They just want privacy and to take it easy, so you can offer them a hamper for breakfast, and refer them to the pub or your favourite local spots for dinner.

7. Event-goers

What's better than doing one thing you love? Doing three things you love! Event-goers are aficionados looking to follow an interest, and have a road trip adventure with friends. All that, plus they get to enjoy a region. For example, the country horse race circuit, festivals, sports carnivals, charity drives - there's a whole bunch of regional events giving completely new markets a reason to visit to indulge an interest. Events can boost your occupancy and help extend your shoulder season.

Where to get more data about self-drivers

A lot of the advice you get from tourism marketing experts doesn't reflect the reality on the ground. Sadly, there's not a lot of research done on self-drivers outside caravanners and RV owners. Tourism marketing advice is based on research, and research is based on available data, and data can be flawed, aggregated, averaged, or quantitative not qualitative. And if no one is collecting data about self-drivers other than road counters, then by definition you are working in an unstructured, hard-to-define market.

But if you've been observing self-drivers' behaviours, habits and preferences for a long time, you probably know more than most. I have been for about 20 years, and here are some of my reliable sources:

- The Caravan and Camping Industry Association of Australia does great research on the recreational vehicle (RV) market, and collects bookings and occupancy data from caravan parks, where it is evident that for a few years now cabins are providing the most profit and revenue, and are the fastest growing accommodation segment in Australia. To return to my earlier point, there are more people driving around with a mid-price budget, without caravans and not wanting to camp.
- The RTA profiles mentioned earlier have high level data on modes of travel, and if you have a contact in state tourism commissions they often run private research which they are happy to share if you ask nicely and don't spread it around. They also run perception research on different regions, and drill into RTA findings.

But you don't need to dig too deep to understand self-drivers.

They are everywhere, all year round; they have needs, and they have money to spend. This is what regional tourism looks like across Australia, year in and year out. With the occasional HYT (High-Yield Traveller) in there and some backpackers thrown in for good measure, scrambling for cover or, more likely, having the time of their lives.

Why modes of travel matter

Modes of travel matter, because you can tell a lot about people, their mindset and their budgets, by the way they move around, the kind of holiday they have booked or are having. More pragmatically, to get bookings you can start to work out where they are likely to stop, rest, and eat, and if you know that then you can position your marketing and branding at those points - train stations, roadhouses, near National Parks, entrances to the main street, walking trails, or as they leave the airport. Conversely, you can also avoid these places if you don't want this market or want to differentiate.

What are modes of travel?

These include a pretty wild number of combinations when you look at the diversity of options in the travel and transport industry. Other than the straight up self-driver, here are some others:

- **Fly/drive**

The most common combination: fly into a major state or regional airport like Perth, then hire a car and drive, say down to Margaret River.

- **Fly/fly**

This might be a combination of flights, or a major airline and then a smaller regional airline or charter flight. So you fly into Perth, then fly to Geraldton.

- **Drive/ride**

This adventurous crowd drive to a destination or node, get on a mountain bike or a horse or a camel, and do a tour, safari or self-guided trail for a day or more. Then they return to the node and drive on to the next destination, or home, or back to the airport/train station.

- **Drive/hike/climb**

Like the above market, but they use their legs and possibly even climb, hike and abseil. They may also fly in from somewhere else if your local hiking trail or mountain ranges are particularly alluring. This crowd may also fly/drive/climb to pursue their passions.

- **Drive/sail/paddle**

Drive to the water to launch the boat, kayak or board the yacht or cruise ship. Stay on the water for some time to paddle, surf, lounge about or sail. Reach their destination before returning, collecting the car, or being transported home.

- **Train/drive or train/drive/fly**

A retired couple take an epic Australian train journey, and then hire a car in say Darwin and drive around or take a tour before heading home by train, or more likely a direct flight.

There are also ferries, helicopters and buses that I haven't included, but which feature in more established markets. Most of these are private; you have limited to little opportunity to get any free promotion on or near them as it's a pay to play system.

But some public access spaces like trails and National Parks do allow you to position, promote or just think about who is coming past your town, and how they move around. Think it through, and you will find opportunities to engage and get exposure where people stop, plan, eat, fill up with petrol, pump up tyres, buy rope, fix backpacks, enquire about doctors, need to feed animals - you get the picture.

WHO PROMOTES TOURISM IN AUSTRALIA?

There's a lot of focus on marketing in tourism, especially the highly visual campaigns featuring celebrities being 'typically Australian' (and almost always disputed by Aussies everywhere). Being noticed and known by your target markets and sometimes by third parties is critical to being booked. You must be where you can be seen, and I will show how you can do this as you start out. At government level, the budgets are much bigger, primarily to get as many people to look at Australia or your state. Tourism Australia (TA) promotes the whole country to people overseas. We rarely see their overseas tourism marketing because it's targeted in other countries. State and Territory Tourism Organizations (STOs) focus on - you got it - the state and regions in it.

Tourism marketing is generally focused on destinations and 'experiences' that revolve around a nature, culture, adventure theme, or some variation of this. Sailing, eating, drinking wine, hiking, talking to Indigenous people, diving with whale sharks - what an active bunch! If you are someone who prefers being served your meals, shopping for clothes or sitting by the pool, chances are Australia's tourism marketing will not appeal, but a resort in Fiji may. Tourism Australia campaigns put Australia, and maybe your region, in the consciousness of travellers at a very high level in the early stages of their booking life cycle.

How to start marketing

Your job is to make sure your tourism marketing reflects:

1. What is actually available or possible to do within reason
2. People actually doing it
3. In the best light possible
4. So it attracts a target group of potential buyers.

For example, a 4WD tour appeals to lots of people, old and young. Older people may prefer a hosted picnic lunch, to do fewer crazy trails, and sip wine at sunset under the stars. A younger crew of mates on an adventure may be driving more challenging tracks, and hiking up hills to celebrate in a sweatier way. So first you need to understand and research the demographic you are looking for, according to your brand and position in the market.

Know where your visitors come from

It may surprise you, but in Australia most people travel within their own state. This is called the intrastate market. Up to 80% of total visitors are from intrastate. Between 10-20% of the state's visitors come from interstate, depending on where your region is and how close it is to icons, and a smaller number, 2-10%, are internationals. You can see this reflected in the National and International Visitor surveys (NVS and IVS) published each quarter, and in Regional Visitor Profiles published annually on TRA's website.

Unless you are offering a groundbreaking new eco-hotel or 5-star experience worth a day trip from a capital city, generally you will attract people already coming to the region. You can get a feel for this group - or demographic - by reading up on your region's Visitor Profile, a fantastic resource to help you learn the characteristics of current regional visitors, understand trends, numbers, where people originate from, length of stay, and average spend per night. See Resources at the end of this book for the URL to Visitor Profiles.

Marketing structures and how to use them

The rule of thumb is the further away your tourism business is located from a large market where potential holidaymakers live, whether it's London, Auckland, Sydney or New Delhi, the more you can benefit from leveraging Australia's tourism marketing structure. You will find what works best for you in your town or region, depending how your state is organised. For better or worse, each level of government offers support and tools to help you. Below is a diagram of the various tourism marketing structures that provide a framework for the Australian industry. Understanding this will save you a lot of time by not working at the wrong level too soon or too late.

In each state, Tourism Industry Councils represent industry and are excellent for networking, information about Tourism Awards, training and accreditation, industry skills, and workshops. While they are great, they don't often make it to remote regions for face to face events, but digital meetings can keep you connected to the latest webinars and provide opportunities.

Tip: Manage your expectations about what others should do for you, as you may be disappointed, and waste time waiting for them to market your region or business. Many regional bodies lack campaign resources, so it is not unusual to feel you are alone, doing all the heavy marketing, lifting, and waving in your corner. In many cases this is true.

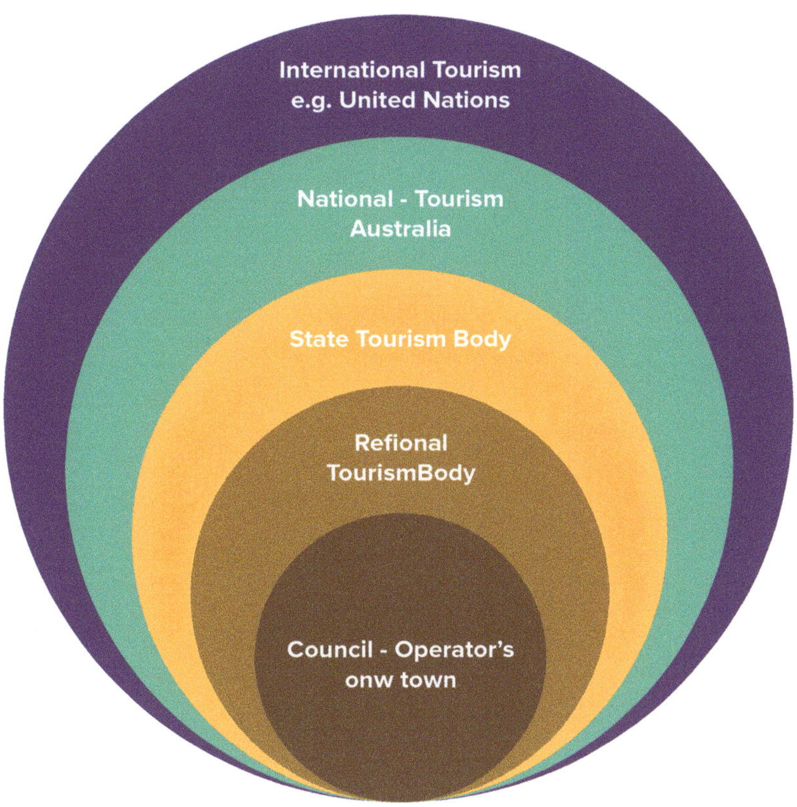

Diagram: The levels of tourism governing marketing of Australian regional tourism businesses

- **Councils and Local Government**

  Some regional Councils may have a Tourism Officer who may publish a local business guide – if so, make sure you are in it! There may be a local government tourism association - LGTA, LTO or some version of them. Depending on the size of your regional Council, it may also fund a Visitor Information Centre (VIC) or a website, or contribute to a regional tourism body (RTO) or employ a manager to promote industry across neighbouring Councils, and manage industry programs or awards. Get to know this person well if you can. Councils may manage a tourism business listing on their website from ATDW, or have some social media including hashtags (#peterborough_sa) that you can use on your posts so your social media accounts are included in any searches - for Peterborough in SA, for example.

  Most regional Councils are not marketing or business growth focused. They are not geared to do it, and if small they generally lack expertise in this area. They have a regulatory role, so will want to check your fire safety plans, pavement advertising, and outdoor dining restrictions set by the liquor licensing body. Some Councils charge a fee for outdoor dining or advertising, which is a shame as these things create a good street vibe and visible open for business indicators to get people stopping and spending.

  After a year or two or more of operating a B&B or café, you will become visible, so expect a letter or soft contact at some point. This is a good sign: it means your marketing is working! Keep your touch light and polite - don't get bogged down in administrivia. Comply with local laws, and you can trade without drama. You want to work with your local community as much as possible, but don't be afraid to ask for things in writing, and why specific requests are being made. You want to know if a complaint of substance has been made formally versus an enthusiastic person getting nosy and nitpicking on your dime.

- **Regions**

  Depending on which state and region you are in, there is normally a regional tourism group, or a Wine and Tourism Association, or some version of this. In populous regions such as NSW, Local Tourism Organizations (LTOs) are funded by multiple local governments, as mentioned above, and in this book I refer to them all as RTOs. Dedicated RTOs are the best starting point as they are connected to state bodies and the local opportunities and news, but some regions don't have any RTOs at all. It can be good to join up to add your voice if you want to raise your profile and get support when the economy is tough, to check in on one another, or rally and apply for a grant to upgrade new infrastructure. Regional tourism groups may also initiate key development projects like a World Heritage nomination, running barista training, even winning grants to rebrand a region where the STO falls short. They are also a great resource for upskilling and networking with people who are already invested in your new industry. In regions, there are also Chambers of Commerce, which are a broader church than just tourism or agriculture, but they charge a membership fee. Check your local group to see their remit before joining though. You want to align with groups who are the go-to for state and federal government when they engage and consult with the regional tourism industry.

> **Tip:** A word of warning: regional committees and volunteering can become draining, and take your focus off your business. Manage your energy levels, and direct your passion into fun, healthy and productive activities that give you joy - or risk burn out, which can harm your relationship, business and customers.

- **States**

  Every state has a tourism commission (STO) or body whose primary job is to market the state's industries. In Victoria it's Visit Victoria, in SA it's the SA Tourism Commission (SATC), in QLD it's Tourism and Events Queensland (TEQ) - all variations on the theme. Sometimes the tourism marketing role is split off from the industry development role as in Victoria, meaning that if you are starting out, you take business advice from one agency and marketing advice from another. STOs work with state and national media, and with regional champion products and experiences, to promote the best of' what the state's tourism can offer to consumers and the media. STOs are a link to Tourism Australia. Some are strictly promotional, while others influence industry development fundamentally with programs, niche market support, and co-funded campaigns with industry proactively targeting niches like school groups or LGBQTI markets.

STOs also have a Major Events arm and fund, and attract star fixtures like the Commonwealth Games, the Masters Games, festivals - conferences that bring special attention and volume to a city, the idea being that some of these visitors will also travel out of the city into regions.

STOs manage grant programs, and design consumer campaigns, often with established operators in regions, offering champion products with marketing budgets. Their role includes infrastructure, making the case for improved access such as ports, harbours, bridges, roads and rail. Build relationships in the STO over time, and welcome a visit from them when they come to the region, or at least attend their functions. Again, build your profile.

> State tourism bodies' budgets vary wildly. They generally work with established businesses with a track record in self-funding their own marketing, and attendance at consumer and tradeshows. Why? Because governments are generally risk averse, and keen to put their best foot forward. If you are new, small or emerging, there is a greater risk in including you in a campaign that you may not be able to service or deliver. I'm not saying you can't; I'm just saying this is the perception, and in the world of marketing that is close to reality.

Generally an STO's focus, unless their remit is running regional campaigns, would exclude small regional tourism businesses for which a turnover of $20,000 to $500,000 is the norm, unless those businesses are paying to participate in a campaign - a great opportunity if you can get it.

- **United Nations World Tourism Organization**

  The United Nations World Tourism Organization is where tourism impacts and benefits are addressed in the context of Sustainable Development Goals, and this is what tourism corporations, hotel chains, airlines, and multinationals use to guide their performance to stakeholders at a global level to tackle issues like poverty, slavery, diversity, and sustainable and equitable travel practices - things that affect us all.

  Tourism Australia and international tourism forums like the United Nations round off the complete structure of the industry. As a new regional tourism business, you will not be dealing at these levels unless you are heavily invested early at scale such as a major hotel chain or attraction and frequented by lots of international markets.

  Tourism Australia is the peak government tourism organisation in Australia, and extremely useful for understanding how marketing works at a macro level when selling Australia offshore. Look at their corporate site Tourism Australia as it has useful statistics, regional profiles, national strategies, and campaign updates, and the Australian Tourism Events calendar. TA are responsible for marketing Australia overseas. They have selected industry programs (such as Signature Experiences, where you see peak Indigenous experiences being promoted globally) that are a way to showcase the best of Australian tourism that aligns with our brand. It's always interesting to see how we are being sold as a country, but the nationwide level of destination branding is complex, and not relevant to your getting your doors open and attracting bookings.

  Also worth mentioning at the national level are multiple peak bodies for industry associations related to the tourism industry. Just for an example the Caravan and Camping Industry Association of Australia has state chapters. Other peak bodies with state chapters include sectors like restaurants, hotels, and museums and galleries just to name a few. You may find them useful for sector specific information, research and technical knowledge, cheap insurance and networking.

Let's summarise

- The 5 Ps of marketing are people, product, price, promotion and position. Working with all of them means you don't need to overspend on promotion
- Practise across all the marketing disciplines to get a complete understanding of the game. Work out what you absolutely need to start with, and what can wait
- 'Free' marketing tools have hidden costs - such as time, and energy to learn new digital or web management skills, manage SPAM, or direct enquiries. If you want to keep your costs down, you need to invest this time, or pay someone to do it for you
- The stages of a traveller's booking life cycle: dream and discover, plan and prepare, book, anticipate, travel, return, and share
- Most regions, especially those without airports or trail access, rely on self-drivers
- 'Self-drivers' include seven distinctive categories, each with its own characteristics such as business markets, grey nomads, visiting friends and relatives, short stay couples, families, 4WDers, and event goers
- Modes of travel can tell you how a person or group moves around a region, and where they are likely to stop, regroup, or be looking for services. They include fly/drive, drive/ride, fly/drive/hike, drive/sail, and so on
- Tourism Australia and STOs primarily fund, create, manage and execute marketing campaigns. Some regions with larger budgets in the RTO/LTO will also run marketing campaigns
- Focus on using your local, regional and state marketing structures when you start out, and connect with TiCs and RTOs for upskilling and networking

Road to Buxton Visit Victoria

CHAPTER FOUR

MARKETING ON A BUDGET

What marketing tools cost, and do you really need that?

The focus on marketing is intense when you start in tourism. More so than many industries, because tourism relies so heavily on visibility, imagery and promotion.

Marketing is a very abstract concept at first that only makes sense once you start doing it, and getting responses. Go with what works. If you are out on your own in a remote region, you may become the town brand, standing out because there's no one else around.

The core question is, how will people find your business so they can book? Visitors are already doing a lot of research, and will find you if you have done the following seven fundamental things:

Seven fundamentals to get booked sooner

1. Budget for your marketing spend

Starting out, chances are you won't have a big budget, so you need to use what's free or affordable and be smart. As a new business, you have to manage your cashflow carefully, and be ready to invest about $2,000–5,000 over a 12-18 month period in things that will set you up for success. Research and create a 12-month plan to help you allocate your funds. Focus on the big items that do the work for you in markets, and give you reach and presence when you can't physically be there.

2. Get a Google account, and list yourself on Google Business

To appear on Google Maps (the red teardrop) you need to have a Google Business account. When your doors are open, get a couple of friends to kick-start your ratings on your profile. Upload photos, your logo, opening hours, phone number. You literally want to be on the map - Google Maps. Don't miss out on low-hanging fruit. People use Google Maps like a guidebook. Being on the map is critical for awareness and bookings.

3. Get a brand, a logo, and a business name that is easy to remember

All tourism businesses need a strong brand (logo, name, colour palette and style), a website and great photos, and simple booking and payment systems. The more digital, 24-hour, book anytime, the better for you - and for them too. A word on names: your grandmother's maiden name from the old country interpreted backwards in code may seem like a great idea (after a few glasses of wine maybe), but it's hard to remember for most, and success in tourism is not just about what you want to do, it's about making it easy for people to find you and book you. In marketing, recall is key, and brands and business names do a lot of heavy lifting. Repetition of your brand - at least seven times - is the hallmark of familiarity and, since we are creatures of habit, a memorable name will help you to be found and booked.

Spend some money on graphic design if you need to. $1,500-2,000 will get you a basic logo if you can't design one yourself using free graphic programs like Canva in the early days. Learn to play to keep it cheap. You need to spend in various areas to start a business, so it's normal to just spend enough to get a basic logo first to get going, then you can always upgrade later when you can afford to and you need better quality. Use your brand on your distribution platforms, ATDW (see below), and your social media and website.

4. Great images of the product and experience

Style and images do a lot of heavy lifting in tourism, so it's worth investing or taking care with this if you DIY with your smartphone. Take or pay someone you know to take 5-6 high resolution photos of your place, tour, or attraction with landscapes, people and great colours for use across all platforms. You can do it yourself with a decent phone. They should be big images, very high quality or high resolution so you can reduce them and maintain quality, or enlarge them on a big screen without their going blurry. Photos should be in focus, and feature people having a good time. Don't cut off heads or hands if cropping, and focus on the experience people can have, not the thread count of your sheets or the size of the mountain bike wheels.

Use the same 4-5 photos everywhere for consistency, and update them every 2-3 years. Pay a photographer and models if you need to, which will cost about $1,000 depending on travel costs and how much styling you do.

5. Build a basic website

This is the most expensive thing you will do starting out, unless you have the time, skill and patience to build your own. Yes, you need a website, and one that is attractive, easy to navigate and ranks in searches when people look online for tours/things to do/ accommodation in your region.

You need to use keywords, and ensure it is search engine optimised (SEO) (see step 7) in the hidden fields or meta tags, depending how your site is built.

For DIY, free to build and cheap to host and register a domain name, SquareSpace, WordPress, HubSpot and Wix are user-friendly platforms that offer functionality with either drop and drag or great design templates. You can also connect a payment system for a small fee (usually a one-off set-up cost and then a % of each sale).

A website developer/designer should deliver a very good, high-ranking website with 5-7 pages, and apply your brand - not just your logo, but matching colours, font and typeface and a fitting layout - for between $5,000-7,000. A web developer and designer will normally charge between $250-400 a year to host your website for you.

Plus, if you add a booking function to take payment securely, there will be an extra set-up and design fee, and the bank merchant services will charge a fee per transaction that you can absorb. These add up, so shop around.

- **Booking systems**

  An e-commerce booking/reservation system will also cost money if you are taking bookings direct or want to use and tie into a third-party booking system like Rezdy, RMS, CloudBedz, E3, FrontDesk, Guesty - there are a lot of options now, so it depends on what your business is and how experienced your web designer is as to how you integrate software.

  The key thing you want on your website landing page is a single reservation calendar that synchronises multiple booking channels (if you use more then one, which eventually you probably will) available dates, and rates. This calendar is critical to avoid double bookings and secure instant bookings.

  Depending on which 'channel manager' you go with you will pay them a commission per booking, around 17% plus a monthly fee from $40 - 65 USD. Sometimes if you hesitate they may knock off some of the price to get the sale. Do an online demo with them to learn software features and get to know the sales person. Tell them you are small, but growing! US companies may be hungry to get into Australia.

  You may not need a booking engine or a shopping cart on your site if you sell indirectly, under contract, or to groups at negotiated rates through a wholesaler, but it's what you do with the site that matters most - just having one won't grow bookings, but it is a start.

Make sure you can manage any content and image updates, and your designer is not using specialised software that's too hard for you to learn to edit. Once you pick a web designer, it's hard to take a website to someone else. You basically need to start again, and that's a big hassle. So pay what you can for a good site early on, and use a capable designer who understands a small tourism business and the industry.

Tip: Master the things you can control, such as your own website, your keyword use, registering with ATDW, being on Google Maps, your images, pricing, and brand appeal. Think about what you are posting on social media, and only do what you can manage to maintain.

6. Register with the Australian Tourism Data Warehouse (ATDW)

ATDW is a singular national tourism database, powering supply of the content for major travel websites including STOs, trade, media and Council websites, Visitor Information Centres and online event listings. Listings get updated centrally by you, the operator, and therefore everywhere else automatically. ATDW has massive distribution and powers searchable content, which means you may also attract some junk email and junk listings.

ATDW needs images of a specific size, and will give instructions as you upload your profile. You can learn to use Canva and do it yourself or you may need to feed a teenager or take an online tutorial to help you crop images to size and resolution to fit properly. Resizing and formatting images is a skill you will use constantly in tourism business marketing!

A word of warning with ATDW. You need to update your listing every 12 months otherwise they will 'sleep' your profile and you won't appear in search bookings on state tourism sites (or anywhere else), even if nothing has changed in your business. From experience, you don't want to learn this in the middle of peak season, trust me.

Tip: People are random, and come through all sorts of channels such as Google Maps, Trip Advisor, Airbnb, third party booking platforms like Bookings.com, and regional websites which don't rely on ATDW. ATDW is a great free initiative, but not the only way to attract bookings.

7. Write a 50, 100 and 200-word compelling pitch about your product

Start by writing up what your experience is, what it includes. Your description will be used over and over again, and should be consistent on digital platforms, social media, ATDW, in emails, fliers and on your website.

- **Sell benefits, not features**

  You should inspire without over-embellishing, and say what it is in as few words as possible. Then you need specific inclusions and features that help people to decide if your tour, accommodation or attraction is for them. It may make sense to pay a writer to do this for you if you can't write it yourself. Many people miss an opportunity to engage and entertain in their copy. This is such an important step because people often talk about their brand new car, bus, or eco lodge without any of the benefits of having the actual experience. "A three-day e-bike cycling tour in wine country" is not as interesting as "Book a nature getaway with friends to this untouched part of the world. Have the night skies to yourself and relax while experiencing the epicurean culture, wildlife and classic wines as you ride the Riesling Trail in effortless style." Writers cost between $80-$150/hr, and a good copywriter should give you a fixed fee for delivery.

  A good copywriter should also be able to help you think through what people type into Google, and direct them to your site. Remember to own your key phrases for your SEO in your content.

- **Using key phrases for SEO**

  If you are doing SEO on your own, at a very basic level, think about the phrases someone is likely to enter into a Google search, and where you want to appear. For example short sentences like 'best thing to do in Katherine with kids' or 'accommodation under $200 in outback NSW', or 'best bakery in Gippsland'.

  Naming your region or a close geographic town (something more familiar to most) can help. Depending how many others are competing in your region for the same market, your search phrases might not be original, but you want to be ranked on the first page of options in a Google search. How do you do this? You need access to the back-end of your website (the content management system or CMS), and find the area called 'metatags', and this is where you enter SEO keyword phrases. Talk to your web designer about which fields in your CMS are the most powerful for search engines to pick up search terms. It's common for headings, page names and subheadings to be beacons for search engines, as well as repeated phrases in blogs.

Digital Marketing

You must have a digital presence in tourism - at minimum a website and some social media to keep your audiences updated on specials, events, and last-minute deals. This is true for most people, unless you are 100% reliant on a distribution platform, or a wholesale arrangement, or have direct niche markets that supply you with all the work you need, or repeat clients.

Sheer population statistics show us that the Millennial generation are large in number, digital natives, and expect things to be online. Eventually they will be making all the spending decisions in businesses, homes, and in social groups including travel. If they can't find it, it doesn't exist. So if this is a market coming to your region, the sooner you use social media the better.

Facebook, Instagram and TikTok are where online eyeballs are.

This said, different demographics use different media platforms. You need to research and understand which demographics you can/want to attract, and where they are going to research their next trip. Do not assume you know.

Once you start, you have to commit to engaging in a sustained way to grow your audience and followers, provided your demographic uses the channels you've selected. Social media is recommended for regional tours, museums, and attractions that keep pace with active city competitors. Attractions and tours need strong visibility to attract group bookings and remain viable. You too must sell tickets and urge people to book online to secure bookings in the region.

The thing about 'free'

A warning about free digital tools: that does not mean fast, easy, relevant or simple!

Digital marketing tools and platforms are not universal, and algorithms change all the time. It sometimes just means you are in a room pulling out your hair, and desperate to pay someone to make it all go away.

Free can be a pain in the butt if you don't have the time or temperament to learn new digital skills. Pay someone, and show them how you want them to do it. Ultimately, your budget and priorities will determine this. There are often courses on digital marketing offered through TiCs and RTOs as core business. You'll learn how to post, what to post, about tagging, Facebook Groups, Reels, resizing images, linking back to your website, blogging, storytelling, making noise - everything. If you need help, pay a professional.

There are plenty of overseas professionals for less than this, or locally based media and marketing undergraduates looking for part time work while they learn. Still, you need to work with them and coach them on your business brand and target markets.

If you are interested in outsourcing, social media four hours a week costs between $400-$800 a month in Australia. Plus, you still have to manage and direct people if you want a return on your investment. Free still means you need to spend time and effort one way or the other, and your time costs money.

Do I really need digital and social media marketing?

A lot of time, resources and energy is dedicated to talking up and teaching social media skills. But if your markets are not using digital channels, you simply don't need as much social media as you may be led to believe. Think it through for yourself. Sit down and write a table out like this example, below, a made-up regional QLD attraction, and identify your market segments by demographic, the rough percentage they bring in, how they find you, and what you can do to reach them.

Market segment	Percentage of your total bookings	Channels they use	How I reach them
Boomers - couples -fly/ drivers	55%	Word of mouth TripAdvisor Google searches Travel section in weekend papers Flight deals ad alerts Webjet Print media Expedia	Join Flight Centre program, or AAT Kings SEO website content Promotions through major local hotels Join Rezdy Give locals discounts, and encourage them to refer friends and family
Young families - locals – self-driving - mums and dads	30%	Word of mouth from friends and family TripAdvisor Facebook Google search	ATDW SEO on our website Facebook/Instagram presence Regional tourism association campaigns VICs
School groups	15%	Direct approaches Google search QLD tourism website Major national tour operator	Direct email with product profile Link to website Meetings Subcontract to major tour company Update Facebook profile

As you can see, many tactics do not rely on your being a social media whizz. As with any marketing plan, it depends on which your markets are as to whether you need a comprehensive digital strategy.

Tip: Yes, you do need a website, but as you will see, there are many ways you can win bookings and be publicised that don't rely on digital tools. You do have to invest in some promotion, but don't overdo it. The main thing is you get started at your budget, and then tweak it as you go. Don't let perfect be the enemy of good.

Anyone who has learnt a new skill mid-life knows that it is not like a duck to water - more like trying to lift baked porridge off an old saucepan: it can be done with patience and a good overnight soak. It is very frustrating if you are not a technical or creative person to face the barrage of comments about how easy it is: "it's free", "here, just do this..." I really empathise with new business owners at this stage. Especially when your to-do list is growing by the day, and you feel that not having a website is holding you back from selling, and bringing in much needed money.

Breathe. Bookings will happen.

Where else should I promote myself?

Be cautious about offers from advertising and publishing companies promising you brand exposure in their magazine, coffee table book, campaign or website. Now that you are on ATDW, and getting your social media brand out there, you are a target for the hundreds of tourism magazines, journals, and advertising companies offering to improve your SEO, profile, reach, and engagement.

There are hundreds of ways to lose money in this industry. You should already be aware of cyberattacks and fraudulent phone calls, and requests by email and SMS, and learn to differentiate between a genuine promotional offer and spam. Then you need to determine if an offer is genuine, relevant, reaches your target markets, and is value for money on a small business budget. Most times it isn't, and doesn't do anything that you can't already do yourself.

Later on, if you want to cement your brand and reinforce it in new markets for future bookings, you may decide to have a photo book made up as a coffee table book, or take part if you are invited to another company's photoshoot featuring your place. For example the Prairie Hotel in the Flinders Ranges is the film and photo location for R.M. Williams fashion catalogues. Then yes, a beautifully made coffee table book for an anniversary event featuring landscapes would be a great idea if the distribution is large and will be sent to your target market (preferably by someone else) in cities far and wide.

In your first years though, my advice is to say no to pretty much everything, and focus on the seven fundamentals in the last section.

Don't be concerned when you Google yourself if your business comes up on online listings for what appear to be tourism wholesaler sites without your permission.

Once you are on ATDW, you are drawn down by hundreds of sites, some that look a bit like online travel agents, which add in your attraction, tour or accommodation to make themselves look legitimate. However, legally they can't sell your services without your permission, so just leave it alone - no point fighting it. They are empty brand shells, attracting advertising revenue but really selling nothing.

Of course if you are being hacked or cyberattacked, report them to ASIC if they are a legitimate company, or your state Office for the Industry Advocate, or Business Affairs for investigation.

Finally, have a website, Facebook or Instagram page with up-to-date imagery and main messages you want to share, as it's these that rank on Google searches. Keep it positive and inspirational, and all the booking information easy to find and click on.

Tip: You must be in multiple places so people can recall you - seven is the average number of times people need to see your brand before they develop trust and recall.

Best Bang for Your Buck

State tourism bodies have access to excellent contacts, media reach and data, but they are not always great at sharing or disseminating them within the industry, especially to newcomers in regions. For any city-based organisation, you will be out of sight and out of mind, so you need to build relationships with STOs when or if they visit regions as they can be valuable at getting you some market exposure and your foot in the door.

The three most useful resources are in the STO in my view, so it pays to work with one or two key people there. In some cases, mostly on the east coast, these roles sit in the RTO if you are in a larger, established region. But the best opportunity for exposure and bang for buck on a budget are:

1. PR/Famils team

Public relations and media familiarization teams look for news stories and angles, for talent and location, the latest product or experience, and new food and wine outlets, but don't often have the budget to get out to regions to meet operators and see for themselves. They are reliant on what they hear, research and see, and what's put in front of them. Do them and yourself a big favour by dropping an email and introducing yourself. Request a meeting with a specific purpose, send action photos or videos, and include them in your social media posts with hashtags (#) using the STO handles.

They can also give you direct advice if something would work for a travel publication, campaign or in a market, so you don't waste your time dreaming up ideas for Condé Nast or Vogue Travel, Caravanning Australia or Gardening Australia magazine. Sometimes they pay for trade journalist delegations to visit regions and write about them, so they might just stay in your accommodation or do your tour, stay at your mini-hotel then write about it, and maybe feature your business. Great exposure if you can get it in a national or even international travel publication. You may offer to co-fund a leg of the trip to host journalists, and hope for a write-up and feature - but usually journos and the PR Famils team can't promise this.

2. Interstate marketing team

Interstate Marketing Managers and teams are excellent sources of intelligence about domestic, national, wholesale, and groups markets that may be travelling in your region. There are loads of niche groups out there (Probus, Scouts, associations and clubs), and some STOs are more proactive than others and may share data with you. All you can do is ask. Their role varies, but they are interested in bringing in school groups, special interest groups, business events, and new trade to your state or territory. Groups markets are essential - if you are an attraction or have many rooms and seats to fill you need volume bookings.

3. Networking with STOs

The other powerful activity you can engage in is networking. Your network is an asset you can call on for advice, support, professional services and collaboration, and it goes both ways. Remember, not everyone will want or can do anything for you, but it's about a web of support and awareness that can really help if you are feeling alone or a long way away from your family, especially if you have moved to a new place to start your dream business or tourism job.

STOs usually host Tourism Australia and international marketing managers for in-person annual updates, which are a fascinating look at what's going on in other countries, how Australia is being positioned, how your state is perceived as a visitor destination, and the offshore campaigns and media featuring your state and region. It's often funny and bizarre, but always fascinating, to understand different cultures and psychology - a bit like seeing how you feature in someone else's dream!

RTOs or large Councils sometimes host key staff in STOs in the region, often the Marketing or Regional Manager, and it's a good thing to make the effort to attend these sessions and industry drinks, and network when you are starting out. It will give you a great boost, get you out among your peers, and build friendships and your knowledge and awareness of who is who and what's going on locally.

If you want to network across the state, join the Tourism Industry Council (TiC), which hosts industry drinks, conferences, and training throughout the year.

It will be up to you to make connections, reach out and introduce yourself, send photos and emails, arrange meetings, use hashtags (#), and tag (@) people in your social posts.

Tip: Be assertive and authoritative - don't feel silly, this is how it's done. Invite people to coffee or lunch, and tell them what you do and what you need... Can they help you, or do they know someone who can? Networking is also about what you may be able to do for them - so remember, give and take all the way.

Ratings and reviews

Reviews do matter, especially when you're starting out. People are influenced by consumer star ratings and reviews - you probably are yourself when you are researching holiday places or restaurants.

So how can you use reviews to your advantage?

In the early days, I advise keeping your prices low, value and experience high, and aim to get around 20 positive reviews at four or five stars. This will bring more people your way, confident you are not a one-hit wonder. Then you can start tweaking price and inclusions to maximise your profit margin without pricing yourself out of the market.

Personally, I don't think it's a bad thing to have a few negative reviews, especially if you manage them well. They show:

a. You are human

b. Some people just like to complain

c. Shit happens. For example, people don't read terms and conditions, and it's how you deal with it that counts

Negative reviews can help you to define your target markets and tweak your communications, price, and brand to attract the right kind of customers and leave the complainers who want it all, but don't want to pay.

As a consumer - maybe you do this too - I look for balance in reviews, and judge for myself if it was just a bad day or a consistent experience.

As an operator, you can encourage guest reviews on Google Business, Facebook, your website, Trip Advisor, by sending people a review link in a follow-up email after they check out. Be ready to manage reviews, and respond in a timely way to any comments, so make a habit of checking your Google Maps business profile regularly (the red teardrop). Be polite and concise in your replies, and never attack or confront - best to stick to facts and pursue any claims in writing behind closed doors.

Awards and Accreditation as promotional tools

When you join a TiC, their services include managing the state Tourism Awards (which lead into National Awards), and the Australian Tourism Accreditation Program - otherwise known as Quality Tourism. These are industry programs, and many operators find them useful. Chances are these programs won't be your first priority if you are a small regional tourism business hustling for bookings, but it's worth considering their benefits.

There is some extra status you can attach to your business as a Tourism Award Winner or Finalist, being accredited, or Eco Certified. If you are in a fiercely competitive region, these can strategically set your brand apart from competitors, not just in your region, but in other regions nationally, as well as standing out to the trade agents and wholesalers who sell your product from competitors all over Australia or even the world. You can possibly even charge a higher price. Your status is a point of difference, and anything that helps you attract attention can win you a booking when it's down to you and one other.

You are already in a natural growth upswing when you are new in the market. Some operators find comfort in following the business planning section in the Tourism Accreditation Program, but in my view accreditation can be a bit paperwork heavy for simple micro and small tourism businesses.

Where accreditation works is for businesses with higher risk, technical or safety regulations like flight charters, animal handling, or using adventure equipment like abseiling. Many of these industries have high levels of compliance already outside of the Quality Tourism program, but in these cases Tourism Accreditation and TiC staff offer advice and support that you can lean on as another layer of risk management to ensure you meet legal and regulatory requirements for safety, licences and insurance. Accreditation documentation also helps to train and educate staff and your business partner if you are scaling. If you are small, what does get measured are safety and hygiene by your Council, but that's a simple matter of dealing with them direct.

Eco Certification

When you hit a flatline in growth - in about year three or four usually – it's a good time to consider something like Eco Certification. A podcast by TIC Tasmania showed consumers are increasingly expecting brands and businesses to be part of the solution for big global problems, and are no longer passive 'pamper' travellers, wanting to escape such things. Responsible tourism is a growing area for future consumers looking to support ecologically responsible operators and nature-based experiences. Awards for eco-tourism bring exposure and branding benefits, and they can help you to propel scaling. Eco Certification is offered through Eco Tourism Australia.

The rule of thumb is, if you are watching your expenses - and you should be - any financial or market benefits of programs should outweigh the cost to you to join, and also manage the additional administration that comes with them. You will judge for yourself over time where to invest for the return it brings among all your other priorities.

Distribution dynamite

One of the best ways to improve bookings is a powerful, reliable, and easy to manage distribution system. What on earth does that mean?

It means having a credible brand to vouch for you, and refer bookings to you from markets you can't physically service yourself. A good distribution system gives you powerful reach without significant time and cost to set up and manage it. The best thing about great distribution is when suddenly things take off without all the heavy lifting. It's exhilarating, and of course you have to set it up right, but when it's done making money feels effortless. Who doesn't want that?

Attractions and tours should take especial notice of this section, as you need volume and foot traffic to make a profit. Distribution is a key part of any promotional marketing, and a secret of successful regional tourism businesses. Most of us have someone else, or many other channels, that bring in customers, and we pay a fee for each and every booking. So they make money and we make money.

For this arrangement to work, the distributor must also make money. This is the agreement - someone is 'clipping the ticket'. Weigh the cost of doing it all yourself versus paying a commission for a large, possibly global, distribution partner or platform doing it for you. Getting 80% of a booking is better than no booking. Just make sure you have a healthy margin factored into your rates before commissions and tax. More information on commission pricing is available to you online at Booked Out! Resources.

For example: If you have only one room in a house to sell at a time, Airbnb is a great distribution and booking system, getting your house out to a wide global market that can book instantly. If you have several rooms for different accommodation types under one brand, you may go with multiple accommodation booking platforms like Stayz, Booking.com or Wotif, where you can sell multiple rooms. Or you may be best with a tailored software solution to help you manage multiple channels, calendars, bookings and emails, including direct bookings. Again it depends on where your market is, and what platforms they are likely to use as to which distribution platform works for you. Most regional tourism accommodation and tours appeal to broad markets not niches, so you want a broad consumer platform used by a wide and diverse group of people.

You may only need one or two distribution outlets though, depending on your business model. You will pay fees for distribution - normally 10-20% commission plus taxes and transaction fees. Consumers pay an extra fee built into the rack rate. Millennials and Gen Ys seem to accept booking fees more than Gen X and Boomers - it's just part of the digital world now.

Distribution chains are a next level investor topic, as that starts to factor in all the agents involved in reaching overseas customers, but the principle is similar if not simpler. In a domestic market, to reach customers located interstate, a distributor – an online platform or a travel agency – will take your product, often with other competitor tourism businesses, to a much bigger market using their own brand, technology and resources to promote you. They make money when you get a booking. They oversee the transaction and invoice the buyer before stepping out, and then pay you once the trip is completed.

Your website is an example of a simple distribution tool. Even an average website distributed well will do better than a great site or product that doesn't get to market. But it is generally hard to get traffic to a small business website. Search algorithms change, keywords change, your competitors may be better at it, your designer may not have keyword optimised pages: there are lots of variables, which is why I don't only rely on promotion for bookings. Using the brand power of distributors whom consumers know and trust is smart, and often not considered until surprisingly late in the game by many small regional operators. Why surprising? Regional communities can be very conservative in Australia, unlike their city counterparts. They tend to adapt late, and if they are only in tourism as a hobby or for retirement income, some of your competitors probably don't think adapting to best practice is urgent. All the better for you.

Now more than ever, you can make money without leaving home. These digital platforms are perfect for regional tourism operators with simple management tools. Use them! The returns are there to be had for those who take risks, and you can benefit by being a first mover in your region. Technology has brought markets closer than ever, reducing the need to travel to city meetings to self-promote. That seems so old fashioned now!

There are many distribution platforms and third-party sellers, and different cultures will be familiar with different apps, sites and booking platforms. Make sure you do your due diligence to avoid scams. Distributors who onsell accommodation, tours and attractions to their members and audiences include well known well-known brands like:

Automobile Associations - For tours and attractions

A great option is to tap into national self-drive markets anywhere in Australia, and encourage members into your state or region. NRMA now has a strong national focus, and is actively selling Australian and Indigenous experiences on their website, and although it is the biggest and best in the field, most states have an Automobile Association doing something similar. Many AA members get discounts on holidays, so you may feature in a campaign if you want to offer a deal they can promote.

Airbnb - for small accommodation operators

Love them or hate them (I love them) Airbnb has an enormous global reach, and a super secure frictionless booking, management, transaction, and reviewing platform for both customers and property hosts. Airbnb charges a commission, around 15%, plus a booking and VAT (tax payable in the US) fee, so it ends up about 20% on top of the nightly fee that the customer pays. I cannot recommend them more highly if you are opening up your farm, shearers quarters, beach house, renovated churches, yurts, caravans, underground bunkers, and heritage buildings for regional travellers. This platform disrupted the old hotel model, made accommodation less exclusive and more diverse, and challenged the role of travel agents, putting the focus back on relationships between host and travellers.

Airbnb is a game changer for anyone becoming a host and wanting to make money fast. The platform has features which enable pet and cleaning fees, or add on other tours and experiences. Customers and hosts are subject to mutual private and public reviews after each booking, creating excellent transparency and accountability, and there's a great dispute resolution and payment process umpired by actual people. Lots of community resources are online for hosts, including details about cancellation policies, and other management tools like auto messaging and remote check-in ideas.

Rezdy - For tours and attractions

I've read mixed reviews about Rezdy, but have included it as they are Australian with some reach into Asian markets, which are increasingly important for Australia and regional tourism growth. Rezdy is for operators running and selling tours, activities and attractions. This company just got bought out by a US tech investor in 2023, so expect to hear more from them in future. Rezdy is not for accommodation operators, but if you run simple accommodation in a region you can get a Rezdy agent QR code and onsell local tours and attractions which are also on Rezdy, and make a 10% commission by helping out your industry. Plus you give your guests an easy one-stop shop booking platform via your website when they are booking their bed night. Triple whammy - tick, tick, tick!

AAT Kings - for accommodation, tours, attractions

Yes, they run big buses, but did you know they have small bespoke tours too? AAT Kings Product Managers are open to packaging quality four-star minimum accommodation for 12-24 people, tours and attractions for their coach and small group itineraries. An Aussie icon, they operate in glorious and often remote areas, where it makes sense for them to support locals so as to give their passengers a wonderful time. Outback Spirit is another coach company operating in many remarkable regions. Look around your region to see who is driving through, and look at their itinerary to see if it's a fit with your tour, attraction or group accommodation (minimum 12 rooms plus one for the driver).

There are many more, including online travel agents (OTAs), but ask your STO or industry connection to tell you which distribution and wholesale partners are working with successful operators in your region. They should be able to give you a list.

Tip: Airbnb also sell Experiences now, so when people book accommodation, they have an option to book local experience. This is a great, low risk way to add value and work with another person locally who might be willing to offer and host a short tour, workshop, food experience or gallery talk. Partnering with others and upselling are both tactics for getting booked out.

Using Price Strategically Over Time

To enter a market, I suggest that you keep your prices low just to get initial and frequent bookings, plus build up some solid ratings, improving things as you go from feedback. Then you can change your price strategy - different rates on weekends, holidays and peak times to reflect the surge in demand and possible lack of supply - when your value goes up. This is normal in tourism.

There is something about being perceived as the best that makes people want it more. Reviews are gold, and trusted by future markets. My aim was to get as many good Airbnb reviews as often as possible to build a profile, and work out what people liked. I used a frequency strategy, kept my price low, and attracted a market that enjoyed what they were paying for. It didn't take long to work - maybe 12-24 months - and I didn't spend a cent on marketing, just took some good images, did some styling in the house, developed a brand name and logo for The Outback Shack, and added some thoughtful on-brand inclusions like good teas and coffee, quality beds, funky cushions, and art work that I update regularly.

Over time, I've upgraded furniture and sheets, and trained my cleaner, and can now comfortably charge three times what I started at. I have a strong market position, attracting higher paying customers, and averaging 4.5 star reviews. My job now is to maintain my position in the market and keep my ear to the ground. Superhost status comes and goes, but I don't really pay it much attention.

For example: Prices may go down over time as new competitors enter the market, but this is not generally a sustainable strategy unless you are offering a range of services at different price points and can make your margin in other ways. Then having a loss leader or low price strategy on a popular tour or a single bedroom can be a great way for a customer to get a taste of your brand at a low price point, and add on other services when there, or come back for the more expensive experience another time.

How do I set my price?

I have two ways of pricing: the first is analytical, but the second is more gut feel. Either way, you need to sit down and work out your direct costs to give you a stick in the sand. Pricing tools are free on my website under www.cvconsult.com.au/bookedout-resources.

Analytical

The first approach is knowing what things cost. You must cover costs and make a profit. This is your base price. Now you really need to know what your competitors are charging and what your customers would pay in their hometown for something similar. What is their normal? Not everyone sees value in the same way.

What is the expected price point for a hotel or attraction entry on par with your tourism idea? It costs $30 for all-day entry to MONA in Hobart, $25 to go to the movies for two hours, $220 for a nice hotel room in a CBD. Backpackers would pay around $45 for a bunk in the Sydney YHA. Do your research and ask around. Get Googling. Knowing these things helps you to understand spending psychology.

Tip: You are not the market, so it's not wise to think, well, I wouldn't pay any more than $80 a night, because – and this is hard to believe when you're starting out – there is a market which will pay more, maybe double, because they don't know your region. They have different values, and the convenience is worth more to them.

After you've done your external market research, now it's time to look at what things are costing you to deliver. This is all about direct costs. I have uploaded a worksheet on my website under Resources for you to work out the direct costs of your product. You need to work out pretty early (before you build anything or open your doors) how many people you need to book, to break-even and what profit you can make at what occupancy? Don't run away, stay with me. This is a big area many operators never bother to understand or completely overlook. And it's not hard. So what are direct costs? These are inclusions like packed lunches, park entry, fuel, casual wages for drivers and guides, cleaning fees, but not overheads like rent, power or insurance. You need to make sure what you are charging not only covers the direct costs, but gives you a healthy margin. It's the margin that pays for all those other bills, and you wages. If you are only just covering your direct costs, you are losing money every time you commit to the sale.

All your overheads (marketing costs, insurance, repairs, travel costs and superannuation) are covered by the margins you earn from each tour, bed night or entry ticket. So your price should be more than all your direct costs, plus a healthy margin, plus GST. If it's cheaper than others, good for you. If it's more expensive, can you do it cheaper by innovating, or are you prepared to be the high-end option? Either way, knowing what things cost is a fundamental of price setting. A basic direct costs worksheet is available under Booked Out! Resources on my website. Now you know this, it's time to work out what the market will pay.

Gut feel

A good friend who ran a very successful luxury tour in the Top End NT taught me this method: the second way to set a price is to say aloud the highest price you can before you feel really uncomfortable and can't even say it out loud - practise saying it: My tour is $680 a day - croak! Then drop it back a little, until you can say it with a straight face. My tour is $550 a day. And breathe. This might not be your end price, it's to demonstrate that we often, women especially, undervalue what we have to offer. But this is what you think you are worth, and you are asking for the market to value you as you do to come on your tour.

People, especially when on holiday, will pay more than you might think. You will only know your product's true value to someone else if you travel yourself and can understand the unique things about your town/region/heritage that others would love. If you can see your unique offer from an outsider's perspective, set it up well, using the fundamentals of a great experience, then, having done your research on what other great experiences cost, you are in a good position to ask for what you are worth. There will be a market that will pay your price, even if others won't. Don't settle for less.

If your pricing strategy seems complex - and it can be - again, this is something CVC can help with. Get in touch.

Discounting

Discounting is different to having a low price strategy. I'm not a fan of discounting as a strategy to compete as it's a race to the bottom unless you know what you are doing. Also, you may be inviting a type of customer who is not be worth your time. Discounting - reducing your rates temporarily - works well at the 11th hour, when you have a handful of remaining seats or a last-minute cancellation, or to improve your margin after you have already covered costs. Then you are not losing anything. But ongoing discounting signals you are not confident of your value, and markets see you as a discount brand and learn not to trust you. Think of those Closing Down rug sales that go on forever, so that you never feel you're getting a deal, and even when heavily discounted, there's a voice saying "yeah, but that seems like a normal price..."

If you are discounting as a way to sell, then perhaps you need to drop your price while you build up value with investments in branding, product, service, and delivery. Then raise your price until bookings start to fall off and you have found the top of your market. Just be careful though, as bookings might be falling off for other reasons outside your control.

Yield vs volume

A lesson I learned early in my career was from Rob Coro, hotelier at the Desert Cave Hotel in Coober Pedy in 2008. Rob was a slightly gruff but often very generous Italian, who said little, ran a lot of businesses, and sat on the outback tourism board I worked for. His father had built the Desert Cave Hotel with above and underground rooms back in the 1970s, and Rob sold accommodation and tours to thousands of tourists around the world wanting to experience this strange Australian opal town in comfort. As an experienced second-generation family outback hotelier, he had seen and heard a lot of things.

When the board was deciding on our target market, I suggested, as was on trend at the time, a higher-yielding luxury market would be good for our region - less of them and more money, right? Environmentally sustainable for the outback? Rob simply replied that "There are more families and people on lower incomes with cars who want to go on holiday than there are rich people who will spend thousands to fly in."

As a marketer, my own logic seemed clear. But now I'm an operator in the outback, 20 years on, and have worked with many regional tourism businesses reliant on self-drivers. I've never forgotten this, and the same sentiment has been echoed by many operators I've met over the years.

Going for high-yield is expensive and risky, but can pay off if you have good distribution and can deliver a consistently high-quality experience. Australian regions, as beautiful as they are, are volatile for many reasons covered earlier on in this book, so consistency is hard to achieve. A region is healthy if it has a range of markets, but, at the end of the day, money is money and a booking is a booking, and sometimes you can't afford to be too choosy about your market. Are you in business or not?

High-yield travellers – a real opportunity or smoke and mirrors?

It's fashionable for government advisers and consultants to support marketing campaigns aimed at high-yield travellers (HYT), and invest limited dollars to compete for wealthy global markets, which costs a fortune. This means some other target markets miss out, or the operators attracting them just take care of business themselves.

I've heard it said by marketing executives that by targeting wealthy markets, it inspires and influences people who can't afford to will pull out their credit cards and book a holiday, even if it's not business class. They spend. As an added benefit, relatively wealthy markets may also consider and book a destination that looks luxe, or up to their usual standard.

This is akin to trickle-down economics which have been disproved widely elsewhere. Also, research has shown time after time that international markets into Australia spend more per trip than domestic markets (a common definition of an HYT), but barely move off the east coast of Australia except to regional destinations with airline connections (and we all know that's mostly the Gold Coast and Byron/Ballina). So one has to wonder, is it really the best use of taxpayer money if you are not in those regions, or would those travellers who do tour come anyway?

Research done in the NT in 2003 by Dr Dean Carson showed the value of self-drive markets was that their spend is widely dispersed into regional and remote communities. So mode of travel - covered earlier - matters in regional tourism.

So be aware when well-meaning professionals justify not investing in self-drive, family market campaigns in favour of targeting high-yield travellers with aspirational campaigns that it may not work at a regional level if you haven't got the right product or access.

The definition of HYT probably needs a bit of attention. Does high-yield mean a market that spends more over the course of the entire holiday or more in a short period of time on individual experiences? The publicly available research we have about spend is in TRA Regional Visitor Profiles, where spend data is broken down in two ways:

1. National data for all of Australia includes international visitors' long-haul plane fare into spend statistics to make the value of the market look big, even though that money wasn't really spent here
2. At the state level, they take the airline flight for internationals off the average daily spend per person.

So we get two different spend numbers for the same group of people. Then there is a market that probably doesn't even register in surveys - they spend a hell of a lot and are just not showing up in data, and they are seriously high-yielding!

Either way, if you can get a market happy to spend more in your region, you'll be doing well!

Few start-up tourism businesses rely only on HYTs, with charter touring the exception when a driver/guide is hired to host people where there are no scheduled public flights.

Where high-yield works

High-yield travellers are an excellent market to get if you can, but not every region is equal as I have covered in Chapter 1 Getting Started. As a general rule, being close to an airport, or within a couple of hours drive at most, helps to attract HYTs as they are usually time poor. However, travelling in private vehicles and jets, this crowd generally don't bump around on rough roads for very long. And it better be worth it when they get there, otherwise watch out!

High-yield marketing strategies work in beautiful places that are hard to get to - think remote lodges in Tasmania, on Kangaroo Island or in the Kimberley - and thus difficult to service because of dirt roads and, typically, hard to maintain due to a combination of factors such as remoteness, cost of contractors from the next major city, seasonality, low populations who may also be unskilled or elderly, or too young to work. Therefore staff is in short supply. Prices are high because food and goods are flown or trucked in, so you need to attract higher paying guests to make it worth doing. It makes sense for these businesses to charge more, because they have to cover costs, and also because the only market that can afford them is a higher-yielding market, looking for something outstanding, different and special. Often these places are seasonal, and so owners can only make money over five or six months of the year.

The power of a new build

If you are in a remote region and have an opportunity to build new, then back yourself because most people underestimate the power of a new building, especially where you can offer a 4-star plus experience, which is in high demand nationally, and lacking in most Australian regions.

Tip: A new building attracts all sorts of people, and delivers interest, awareness, and more reasons for other businesses to invest, thereby attracting workers and families. It helps keep regions alive, although it is not the building itself that makes money, but the experience on offer.

So do your homework and make sure it stacks up and is feasible. If you are looking for further support in this area, Tourism Infrastructure Advisory is a service my business provides for bespoke accommodation and trails.

Work with the weird traveller mindset

Up with distribution systems that can deliver easy bookings, acknowledging the weird traveller mindset is another favourite way to make money in tourism and increase bookings. I love it because I recognise it in myself, and you may too.

Travellers have different needs

Something weird happens when we exit our ordinary and hit the road. We spend more, we eat differently, think differently and react impulsively when exposed to new things. A friend of mine buys pickles, preserves and jams every time she visits Adelaide, but doesn't when she's at home in Sydney. She gives them away. I'm a sucker for a quirky tea towel or a quality t-shirt featuring a destination. Another friend always buys the book after seeing a blockbuster exhibition.

Now we are entering the weird traveller mindset. This is where you need to get out of your own world and play with peoples' perceptions to see how you can simplify things and offer new services to make extra margin. You may be very surprised at the things people pay for.

Travellers will often be willing to accept things on holiday they wouldn't at home

When we travel, often it's to experience another part of ourselves. We think we are getting away from it all and finding new places, and willingly project a lot of fantasy ideas onto new towns and accommodation. It's exciting, and we are primed to enjoy it from the whole research, booking, anticipation cycle that started weeks, even months before. So as long as you are doing all the basics right, travellers are already 80% convinced they are going to have a good time. Most will enjoy what you've got to offer as they are open to new experiences. So you don't have to try as hard or invest as much as you may think, but you do need to be responsive, and reinforce their perception of your place as cool, great, perfect, amazing with upbeat messages of your own during interactions with customers.

Less is often more

Have you ever walked into a room that is beautifully and simply decorated with wooden floorboards and a breeze lifting the curtains, and just relaxed instantly? Have you ever had a receptionist hand you the keys and say everything you need is here, just ask when you are ready. And leave it at that? No special instructions, fuss or bother? If you are busy, stressed out or in demand, being left alone can feel like luxury. Being in a beautiful place and having less interference means less to focus on and worry about. Your mind can unravel and finally relax. This is an experience many people are willing to pay thousands of dollars for in remote safari camps and simple eco resorts. Throw away the old fridge magnets and shelves stuffed with pamphlets friends have brought back. Create space for the new to occur again and again.

They are paying for you to care, but not bother them

Some travellers don't want to engage and communicate. They are independent. Less communication and fewer tips may be better, as you may be raising irrelevant or unimportant subjects - so why fuss? Give people what they need, like directions, and tell them what to bring, but generally leave it to them to explore, ask you, or discover a place on their own. It's part of the adventure, and also what matters to us does not always matter to them.

Let's summarise

- Many of the essential tools you need to market yourself in the first years are free, including getting on Google Maps, joining ATDW, and opening a social media account
- Yes, you need a website but don't overinvest until you know what your distribution strategy is
- Digital marketing is a must, especially for tours and attractions and multi-room/site accommodation. You have volume to fill, and younger demographics rely on digital more than Boomers and older
- Best bang for your buck starting out is your STO, especially the PR/Famils team and Interstate Marketing Managers, and free networking events
- Ratings are a great way to attract bookings, instil confidence in buyers, and get ahead of competition by showing you are established and can take the good and the occasional (hopefully) bad review
- Tourism Awards and various Accreditation programs can give you a point of difference and profile in the market, best used when you are coming out of the start-up phase if time and budget are limited
- In accommodation, aim for frequency in bookings early on to get reviews to establish your brand. Then consider your price to make sure you are making a profit, not just covering costs
- Distribution platforms are a powerful way to reach new markets without leaving your region, and to attract bookings sooner
- You can charge for services people don't want to do themselves when travelling, such as food packs and booking tours on their behalf
- High-yield markets are often a target for remote tourism products based in hard to reach, therefore more exclusive, regions. These businesses have more risk and higher costs, and need good air and/or road access
- Be confident that less can be more. People are often willing to pay for things that you wouldn't

Hilltop Retreat, Willunga Hill SA. Lost Retreats

CHAPTER FIVE

Welcome to Planet Tourism

BREATHE

Starting a new regional tourism business can be overwhelming.

You will have a long to-do list, and probably be travelling a lot, getting to know useful people in your town if you are new, or the next town, coordinating meetings with tradespeople, staff, designers, your accountant, advisers, and hosting the regional tourism manager. Getting through this period, your mental and physical health is paramount. Staying grounded as you start out will help you to overcome obstacles, let go of non-essentials, deal with gatekeepers, and master new skills.

Don't forget to breathe and enjoy the journey!

Here are some common issues you may encounter, and some tips as you arrive and get settled on Planet Tourism.

Stay connected to your purpose

The tourism industry can be overwhelming. It's broad and deep with lots of sectors, levels, organizations, peak bodies, operators, and so on - also a lot of opinions! Whom to believe and follow? From the outside it seems everyone is having fun and working hard, so you may feel like a little fish, and that's absolutely fine. In fact it can be more fun than a big fish with lots of staff, overheads, and complex investments. Knowing your purpose, and using the power of your breath can help you stay connected when things get busy. Your purpose may not be money. Your business may be more of a sharing of knowledge, a mission, your passion, even a spiritual exercise, but your purpose may change and evolve over time as you do.

Every ecosystem in nature and business needs the little fish, and you can do very well in a niche that bigger firms cannot provide. Little fish become medium fish or even big fish, but it doesn't matter if you never get to be a big fish. The main thing is that you get started, know your risk appetite, stick to your budget, have fun, and learn how other operators ride out the waves. You can learn to surf too.

> **Tip:** Your business will be shaped by the various crises that hit tourism in Australia, and you will need to adapt to keep going. It may end up being different to how you first imagined, but stronger if you don't overinvest early in stuff that doesn't matter, and focus on the things that do.

How much should I engage with the industry?

As a sole trader or micro business, you are often working alone, so the need to network and connect is real. It can be quite lonely in regional tourism. Perhaps this is why the industry loves to network, and RTOs often hold information and training events for operators. I encourage it, and it can be very beneficial for your growth and sense of community.

In some remote regions, there are very few opportunities to get together with your new industry colleagues whereas others seem to have something on a weekly basis! As an exploration exercise, networking is excellent for learning about regional, state and national tourism marketing campaigns and where, or if, your region or product fits. However, a word of caution. Some RTOs can be political and critical of the government or the latest campaign, so watch your energy and alliances. It's easy to lose focus and get distracted or depleted by negativity, and other people may be more established than you, with the time to fight battles that you as a start-up don't have. Manage where you put your energy and time. Find out what works for you.

Many operators don't engage much or at all with official support networks, follow their own instincts and still do pretty well. You don't need to be a member of anything to be in the regional tourism industry or run a successful business. But down the track, RTOs can help to vouch for your credibility should you want to expand your markets or apply for a grant, an award or accreditation.

Use the power of your breath

You may be feeling overwhelmed at this stage - there's so much to learn on Planet Tourism! Knowing how to manage energy is a secret of successful people. Do you ever wonder how they keep going in the face of it all? Mastering the essentials of business includes understanding ourselves, and what is more fundamental than breath? Breath is life. When we are overwhelmed or just out of our depth, our breath gets shallow or jagged. We sit hunched at a computer for hours, or in the car, mind racing, going from one thing to another, and not taking a conscious breath until we fall into bed.

As a business owner, you will soon be busy with a long to-do list. When you feel overwhelmed, remember to breathe. Success does not come overnight. You may not even know what success looks like yet - it is not always about money. In times of uncertainty, it helps to have something simple to ground us, wherever we are. The great thing about breath - apart from the obvious – is that while you are alive, you always have it with you, and it is a great tool to get inside your body, get grounded, and calm your racing mind.

Another reason to take time out and connect with your body and breath is so you don't burn out and can learn to relax frequently, to go the distance, and take stock and enjoy the journey. You want to stop regularly and connect to purpose - and disconnect from the noise and anxiety that come with comparing yourself to other people - the self-doubt and stress of learning to do new things, especially as an adult - it ain't easy! You want to actively bring down your cortisol in the early days so you can function, make better decisions, and respond better to your staff and customers.

So how do you do this?

Yoga

If you are lucky enough to have one in your town or region, a good yoga class will teach you to slow down, reconnect, and move and breathe fully, stretching your lungs and muscles in different directions to increase blood flow and oxygen in areas we don't usually use. This can be very uncomfortable, but it teaches you how to stay calm in difficult situations, and increases your resilience in tough times - something we can all benefit from.

Meditation

Or you can simply sit for 10 minutes each morning and night before you go to bed. Set your timer, and make space and time a priority. Your family will notice the difference, as will you, in a matter of days. There are some good, simple, free guided breathing resources on You Tube, and free apps you can download on your phone – though maybe not while on those long country commutes. See the Resources section in the back of this book for more and also on my website at wwww.cvconsult.com.au/bookedout-resources

Learning how to breathe in times of stress is a game-changing skill, which will support you in many areas of your life.

After all, you are in tourism where people are being encouraged to gear down, step off, relax and recharge. Is there anything worse than being greeted by a stressed out host?

Simplify your focus

To regain a sense of control when overwhelmed or confused by contradictory information, I go into simplification mode. I like to strip it right back and ask:

What is within your control?

What can you do today?

What is your priority?

There is a time for action, but when you look at what is under your control you will see - with relief - that there is only so much you need to deal with immediately.

> **Tip:** Step back once a week and set priorities if you are getting overwhelmed, and avoid the need to fix it or be constantly 'doing'. You will be more calm, grounded, and effective as you go about your tasks, and make better decisions.

Locus of control and locus of concern

This exercise is called determining the locus of concern (all the stuff you are worried about), and the locus of control (the few things you can actually control). The concept is from the *7 Habits of Effective People*, another great book on self-mastery.

It's a helpful way to separate yourself from all the big picture anxieties that can creep up on you, so you can get on with your days dynamically, make better decisions, and enjoy the ride. After all, it's tourism - and if you're not having fun, your guests and staff won't either.

The graphic below shows the elements that regional tourism operators are in control of and what they're not:

Locus of Control: My response, my attitude, my prices, my budget, my plan, my garden, my relationships, my property, the service I offer, my advertising , my time my energy.

I'm not in control of

Who gets funding support

How the government spends its money or allocates grants and contracts

Whether other people think my business is worthy or not

Whether people have a good time with me

What the community thinks

The popularity and awareness of my town or region - this is a collective responsibility

Whether people return or tell others

How much water, power, gas customers use

People's behaviour once they are with me

The quality of my workforce and staff

The availability of staff

The weather or pandemics

Laws and regulations, including Council safety rules and inspection requests

Tradespeople's rates, availability or travel costs

Taxes.

I am in control of

How the business looks and sounds on social media and external marketing

Asking advice from the people around me

My visibility to others and my key markets

Making sure guests have all the information, services and basic things they need when they need them

Making it as easy as possible for people to get on with their holiday and have a good time

Setting up my own and other people's expectations early and honestly

Giving it my best, and regularly reviewing what I'm doing

Fixing things I know are broken

Answering enquiries in a timely way

Whom I employ

My self-respect

Meeting safety regulations and minimising risks

Checking on staff and paying them the standard industry rate or better on time

Contributing positively to the community and the industry

How I engage and support other operators

Paying my bills on time

Where I hide the keys

Whom I let onto my property

How, when and if I engage with others

My attitudes

What I think and believe

How much I spend, and what I spend it on

Getting the facts from my accountant

How I manage my feelings and respond.

And there's another element to this - what you can influence if you have the time.

What I can influence

People deciding to book with me or not – with more information or a deal/offer

People's expectations of my business - unreasonable or not - with kindness, facts, and alternatives

Perceptions of my town/region by running the best tourism business I can

Whether my staff want to continue working for me

Positive reviews by customers on key sites

Referrals

Third parties recommending me

Coverage in the media

Exposure by entering for awards.

That's about it. It's a short list.

Everything else is a second or lower priority.

Existential overwhelm

There are many things that can distract you from simply running your regional tourism business. In particular, growing awareness and concern about climate change, and the increasing frequency of floods, droughts and extreme weather in Australia. Rising energy costs and high carbon emissions from long-haul travel and extravagance also contribute to anxiety. You may stop and wonder how you can do better, be a part of the solution?

Yes, the tourism industry does endorse and propel increased movement, and use of fossil fuels and energy, as well as impacts on community, infrastructure, and natural environments and wildlife.

What do you do to address this, to be a responsible tourism operator? These issues seem so big when you are setting up a farm stay to attract a few visitors during the school holidays to pay your kids' school fees. How do you explain what you are doing on a farm, in your community, or on your tours to combat climate change responsibly, respectfully including Indigenous culture, and caring for the land? Yet this is what consumers are increasingly interested in learning and witnessing.

You may start to feel the weight of this crushing against your own values, shaking your confidence, your purpose. Rather than feel helpless, focus on what you can control in your own life and business. If these things are worrying you:

- Talk to your customers about what you are doing in the tour business
- Make any changes in your tourism experience an authentic point of difference
- Plant a native garden
- Pay to separate and recycle consumables, and pass a small fee on to guests
- Promote the local gardening shop and nature trails
- Build your role in the community, and engage with the people you support and employ
- Learn about the traditional owners of the land where you work, and to speak their language, and share resources in your visitor information pack.

You are not responsible for the whole world's problems, so don't let people dump them on your doorstep, and be clear about where your responsibility stops. Regain a sense of control and calm in what you are doing, and why you are doing it. Pausing and reconnecting with your values is a worthy business and life goal. Also, your guests will love it.

TOURISM SUCCESS FACTORS

Running a regional tourism business (any business really), there are some fundamental principles to remember, even if tourism is not the only way you or your family generate income. Lots of regional farming families diversify into tourism as a hobby, and it can rapidly grow into an important revenue stream, but by treating tourism like a hobby you can easily create misperceptions about what good performance looks like when it is assessed through a business lens - and this can be a shock. This is a performance book for beginners, so I will introduce some concepts now to show what we mean by business performance as you grow into a successful operator. I advocate for tourism as more than a hobby, mainly for regional sustainability and because:

- It helps keep jobs in regions
- Gives kids an alternative to mining or farming
- Being profitable and having a buffer means you can ride out the hard times that we know are coming
- You can consciously invest when others cannot, giving you a stronger competitive platform
- At some point you will start to wonder if we could do this better
- If you don't take your business seriously you will miss opportunities to invest and improve your position when you do have the energy and resources
- If there's a market that wants what you have to offer, it's a great feeling to make an independent living from it for years to come so you can retire in comfort

The four fundamentals of business

1. Your job as a tourism operator is to problem solve to reach a market interested enough in what you're offering to pay you and complete that transaction
2. You need to deliver the goods, and then of course you need to deliver the goods in the best possible way, within your budget and taking care not to over - or under - deliver
3. In business it is about spending less than you make, and investing profits to get an ongoing return
4. As the business owner, you get paid last, after you pay for upgrades, staff wages, insurance, bills, commissions, and of course taxes

Know your endgame

Endgame? What endgame? I hear you ask. I only just got started!

Sounds crazy, but as we are talking about performance, take a step back and consider the big picture. How will you leave your business, and when is that likely to be? What is your strategy, your plan? Otherwise, you may be left wondering how to retire or sell after building a lot of value over many years. Not all businesses last forever, and most regional tourism operators have no endgame from the beginning.

Essentially, there are two main ways entrepreneurs approach making money, with distinctive exit strategies where the owner is paid at different stages. These are:

- **Invest, grow and flip** - Buy a business with untapped value, build it up, maximise revenue, then, in say three to five years, sell it
- **Build and live off the fat** - Start a business with your skill or asset like a house or tractor, pay yourself as you go, live off the earnings, and then close it down when it's time to retire. Most start-ups run this way

The first way, people buy businesses, improve them, then make their money on the end sale. They don't take high wages from the business while it is growing. They set a three-to-five-year endgame to get it up to maximum efficiency, and invest in the key areas such as branding and point of sale systems to ensure a steady stream of customers and bookings. They then sell the business at a profit, and the next person takes it over to improve it in a different way.

This way of thinking is completely different from that of a start-up, or a builder or tradesperson making a living from a skill or qualification, or an asset at hand like a property or family hotel. Most of these businesses have no endgame. They keep going until the owner retires. They take the value out of the business while they live in the form of wages, and maybe sell off a few assets, but rely mostly on the skill of the central person.

Both are legitimate, but it's good to be clear about which you want to follow as it will make a difference to your viewpoint and attitude from day one. Do you plan to sell your regional tourism business at a profit? How little do you need to live so you keep the profits in the business, or do you plan to take a wage from the business early on? How much do you need to invest initially in booking systems, marketing and staff?

Talk to your accountant from the start about setting up your books to reflect the strategy you'll take.

Business success shapers

There are two key aspects in a regional tourism business that affect your chances of success. These are:

Internal factors

The five key internal factors of a successful regional tourism business are:

1. The product, experience or service you sell
2. Frictionless, efficient payment and scheduling systems
3. Forward bookings, and a steady stream of customers
4. A good layout in a physical space, and/or quality equipment
5. Trained staff and/or reliable contractors

This is where most of your attention and locus of control should be.

External factors

External factors play a big role in regional tourism: how people find you, see you, and move around the destination. Here are four external drivers necessary to support a small regional tourism business:

1. Enough year-round demand for your product
2. Awareness of your location, region or town
3. Multiple transport options for access, hopefully in the form of a regional marketing campaign
4. Complementary businesses like tours, cafés, a supermarket, restaurant
5. Stable local economic and social conditions

Having activities and other businesses around your site helps to keep visitors local, making it a more interesting, welcoming destination. More about this in the next chapter.

Location, location, location

Your business location, geography, and proximity to population centres will influence the likelihood of success, and these things are largely beyond your control. So consider population and accessibility. Are you close to a regional centre or town? How do people move through the town - do they drive, walk or ride? If you are in a thin market or a very remote area, you will need to develop strategies to increase foot traffic and get more people to congregate at or near your business. Or you may look at a HYT market, as discussed earlier. For example, holding a series of events throughout the year, or running multiple businesses like a restaurant, service station, motel, tour booking desk, and post office all under one roof are common tactics successful regional operators use. You may need help from your local Council, business group or progress association to help you plan and promote events and then realise them.

> **Tip:** Before you rush headlong into your dream, consider if your site will support your ambition of running a tourism business. What are the limiting factors? Is the site visible? Is there enough buzz throughout the year? Can you add more services to get economy of scale under one roof?

Staying alive is not 9-5

Someone tell Dolly. Running a successful regional tourism business is not 9-5.

In this industry, to succeed over the long term opening on days everyone else is having a holiday is essential. Your perspective needs to move from yes, a public holiday, I can relax to ok, a holiday, more people are out and about, and I want to capture foot traffic. Should I work these hours, or pay my staff time and a half? If you close your doors on public holidays, then you are either not making enough profit to cover these important trading days, or not committed to investing in marketing to the visitor. This sounds harsh, but the people who stay open get a better reputation over time. Even if there's no one around, you have a massive opportunity to market in advance so that you capture any trade, especially if there is no other competition locally. You're it. It may not be your best trading day, but make sure the 10 that did come through love it, and have every reason to spend money with you.

In many ways, you have to step up your game on public holidays because you are more exposed, which also means more visibility, more reward if you get the service right, and people remember you were open when others weren't.

Commitment as a competitive edge

Here is an advanced lesson from experienced tourism operators and not something many people think about when starting out. I have added it for those of you wondering what 'good' looks like at the established end of the sector for operators who are actively capturing international visitors or invested in high-yield markets.

By creating a reliability factor, people remember you being open when others weren't, and they are more likely to return if they are a local intrastate market, which most regional visitors are. Depending on your region and location, you may have international markets. Many international tourists use travel agents to book their holidays because of the risk factor, and the time involved to research. Agents build itineraries for their customers based on their wishes, a bucket list trip of Australia, camel tours, wildlife experiences, walking in nature, shark diving, oyster tasting in the sun. They will sell whoever is open if you offer the world, but if you are not open on the days their clients need it, you'll lose not just that opportunity but many others. And you won't even know. Agents rarely go back if you were closed when they needed you open to give someone the trip of a lifetime.

International visitors – well many visitors – travel at holiday times: Christmas, Easter, New Year's Eve. They don't want to sit in their rooms waiting for you to finish your day off. Also, many of them don't celebrate the Anglo-Christian calendar. They have limited holiday periods (many Americans and Asians only get one or two weeks annual leave), and have spent thousands to be in Australia, in your region. If you are not open and someone else is, guess what? They get the business.

> **Tip:** Agents book holidays in advance for their markets. There is a wealthy market that relies on agents, so they have a lot of influence over their customer base. Agents rarely go back if you were closed when they needed you open to book someone the trip of a lifetime in your region. So you don't just lose once, but the repeat business too.

Commitment provides stability, and makes you more attractive to your industry peers, agents, and marketers so they can reliably sell you. If you can build this into your mindset and actions, you will reap rewards over time.

For more about getting export ready, see your State Tourism body or the Australian Tourism Export Council which run workshops and sessions with industry about minimum requirements to attract inbound markets.

This wraps up the main factors that contribute to the success of a regional tourism business.

Let's summarise

- Identify and stick to your purpose to keep motivated through hard times
- Self-management is a secret weapon of successful people, and managing your energy is fundamental to going the distance and enjoying the ride
- Practising breathing, yoga, and meditation for 10 minutes a day can reduce stress and relax your nervous system if you are getting overwhelmed
- Work out what's within your sphere of concern, your sphere of control and your sphere of influence
- You can work with or around both the external and internal influences impacting your business, often to your advantage
- How you set up your business will affect how you leave, so while you are busy creating value for your customer, consider if you want to take out profit as you go (pay yourself) or when you sell (keeping equity in the business)
- Location, commitment, and consistent opening hours are success factors for a regional tourism business

Woody Island Eco Tours, Tourism Australia. WA Image library

CHAPTER SIX

Destinations, Products and Experiences

WHAT IS A DESTINATION?

In this chapter we look at the links between destinations, products and experiences, because as a regional operator this is your locus of concern and control (see Chapter 4 for more on this concept). If you can get your head around these concepts, you can influence your customers' experience for the better, attract more bookings, and perhaps find better paying markets.

Understanding destinations is a huge part of knowing where and how to invest in your brand, signage, imagery and website content. Your business is like the core of an onion, with many layers between you and the chef's knife. The knife is the customer. You want that knife in the centre - you want the sale. All you have to be is the core of the onion. True to the onion. Be the onion.

But where does the chef go to buy the onion? She goes to a supermarket - the destination. The supermarket is doing a lot of work, directing the chef to the fruit and vegetable section with signage and bright lights, then past the potatoes, and voila! To the onions. If it looks like an onion, smells like an onion, and is sitting among all the other vegetables, the chef chooses that onion. Bang. You get the booking.

In the same way, a tourist is shepherded to a state, to a region, to a town, to your business (the onion) to have an experience. This signalling and shepherding is done via marketing campaigns, infrastructure, trails, signage, signals and referrals.

Often, once you have done your work, you just need to get out of your own way, and let these other levels work for you. Or lobby the local Council to improve them, and therefore your town's chances of being an attractive destination.

In many cases, people are already coming your way, and you just need to be there, be open and ready to engage, and make the sale. So being true to your destination brand, if there is one, even hamming it up a little, can work wonders.

Destinations can be countries, cities, regions, even businesses or attractions such as theme parks, national parks or shopping centres. When you think of a destination, for example Fiji, certain images come to mind thanks to well-funded government marketing campaigns. This is also true in less fortunate times for destinations like Ukraine, where we are now exposed to daily media reports of war. Both are destinations, and both have different levels of attraction to a tourism market. In tourism, the word destination takes on more of a marketing vibe, suggesting both a journey and an arrival point.

Regional destination branding

There's more.

While countries are known for key features (Australia for beaches, and natural landscapes, New Zealand for adventure tourism, Italy for food and Roman history), regions also have their own brand as a destination. The Barossa is a nationally and internationally known wine region. The Australian Alps, the Kimberley, the Red Centre and the Gold Coast conjure up particular landmarks, states and experiences for most Aussies. We know immediately where they are, thanks to years of advertising campaigns, magazines, travel documentaries, or perhaps visiting with family on school holidays. States are also destinations, and have their own destination brands, promoting strengths like regional appeal, landscapes, and things to see and do.

Regional tourism destination branding appeals to the inner desire of a consumer group, and tries to marry it up with what the region offers innately or through the industry – this is how tourism branding works. Campaigns and imagery have an aspirational pull, a dreamlike quality recalled. Then destinations make it to a consumer's shortlist, depending on what sort of experience they want. This is how experiences, products and destinations are linked. If the consumer is into the outdoors and likes an active holiday (experience), they may consider ski resorts (product) in Mt Hotham, Japan, or New Zealand (destination). If they want a cosmopolitan city break (experience) and love arty neighbourhoods, eating out and grungy bars (products) they might look at Melbourne, Barcelona or New York (destinations). If they've seen Sex in the City and now fancy a remote luxury experience in a desert resort or on a camel safari (products) then it's northern India, Dubai or outback Northern Territory (destinations).

A tourism business can also be a destination - especially popular attractions like Scenic World in the Blue Mountains, or destination hotels like the Versace Palazzo on the Gold Coast, or spectacular natural destinations like Wilsons Prom or Budj Bim in Victoria. A destination is usually a physical place you arrive at and spend time (and money) in. People experience the destination through interacting with the tourism business's services, grounds, buildings and staff.

Who is responsible for regional branding?

Destination branding is normally the remit of the STO, or the regional body if big enough with its own budget, or some combination of the two. It belongs in the locus of concern for most operators, but everyone is rarely happy with the final result, and there are always critics or those who feel left out.

However, the job of destination branding is not to keep regional operators happy. It's to communicate something clear, true and real about a place to the people most likely to want it. Then, once heads are turned, all the other marketing layers come into play to hold attention and draw people down a funnel through decision-making to convert into bookings. Your job as an operator is to connect your own business brand to the bigger wagons so you can get exposure to target markets. You will be busy enough converting consumer intention into a booking with a compelling offer, the right price, and being available on the right channels.

In a nutshell, this is the role and structure of regional tourism marketing, and why it matters for your business.

Destination downers

Some places, no matter how you market them, are simply not tourism drawcards, but this does not mean there is not an investment case. In fact, there may be a very good case for new hoteliers and shop owners to work in a less than desirable destination to service a business market or visiting friends and relatives. Destinations don't always have to be appealing to run a successful business, and they do have reputations that can be ruined by terrible events, media coverage, and natural or man-made disasters. Places like Snowtown in SA and Barrow Creek in the NT are tarnished because of the terrible murders associated with them, even though the murders didn't actually occur in those towns. Such is the power of media coverage - it's not fair, but it is real. Unless you are starting a Morbid Murders tour, these towns are unlikely to become thriving tourism destinations. It's very tough, but shows you how important perception is in business, for better or for worse.

Destination design - the Five As

You may wonder what makes some places seem to do better than others? Possibly it's because they have many or all of the main factors that make up a successful destination, and have them all humming nicely, working together. So what are these factors?

The Five As is a tourism development framework I've been using since 2003 that you can apply in your town to see what the bones are in your destination. How well is it working? Why is this? There are often structural reasons. You may want to use this framework to assess tourism limitations before you invest or do any marketing. I use it with development teams in government and place managers in Councils to explore how many opportunities a destination has or can create with a range of coordinated infrastructure and services to attract various types of visitors and more bookings for operators.

A destination is created with Accommodation, Attractions, Activities, Amenities, and Access. Having most of these As in place is an indicator that a destination can reasonably attract a range of markets. In more detail, the five As are:

- **Accommodation** - places to stay at different price points, campsites and cabins
- **Attractions** - things for people to see such as waterfalls, views, visitor centres
- **Activities** - things for people to do such as walking, riding, eating, shopping
- **Amenities** - toilets and showers, Wi-Fi , a café
- **Access** - vehicle access, flight or foot or bike. Access also extends to designing places for people with disabilities, worth considering as 20% of Australians live with a disability, and also want to travel, and like to take holidays

If things are resonating really nicely at a destination, chances are there is branding alignment between these 5As. Often this happens in a completely accidental way, but planning it will hasten the destination's appeal. In other words, the activities line up with the accommodation and target markets that are most likely to enjoy them. For example, hikers (activities) and bike packers will probably enjoy clean but simple cabins (accommodation) in an out of the way place connected to nature, and a network of trails (access) that take them past coffee shops, heritage sites (attractions), and supermarkets (amenities) to restock. A luxury market may rely on airports or rail (access) with transfers to collect them (amenities), to stay in five-star accommodation with activities such as immersive day spas in nature, local gourmet food, and visits to artistic shops.

Responsibility for the 5As rests between the government and the private sector. If you don't have at least three out of five in your town or region, chances are your destination may struggle to attract enough people, or when you do, struggle to keep them lingering and spending longer.

Tip: Download a free DIY Destination Audit tool from my website, that I developed to assess and score the 5As in your town, park or region. Do this with a friend or colleague to be objective about what you've got and how effective it is, then tally your scores to see if your destination is emerging or established. If you need help to interpret the scores, or want to take this up as a more serious exercise across a region with multiple destinations, CVC can help tailor the framework, so you have a great starting point for future development.

What is a product?

Products are what you sell direct with the help of a reservation or booking system (Rezdy, Booking.com, Qantas, Expedia). Product categories in travel include accommodation, tours, experiences and activities, and transport (flights and car hire). Products can be packaged together (ferry transport, galley entry and three course lunch) or with other people's products and sold as an experience. Common examples of packages are: lunch and a show, a hire car and a room, a flight and a room, a tour, dinner and a room.

In this book I focus on tours, accommodation and attractions, and within these categories, there are subtypes. Here they are in more detail:

Accommodation

The greatest visitor spend after flights is generally on accommodation. Even on an overnight tour, accommodation can be a big item. Accommodation has many subcategories such as:

- **Campsites** - powered and unpowered
- **Glamping** - for a higher fee-paying market, cabins or semi-permanent safari tents, often in remote places
- **Hotels** - from 3-star highway inns to boutique 10-room properties
- **Caravan parks** - powered and unpowered sites, camping, and sometimes all of the above
- **Resorts and lodges** - for backpackers, groups, specialist activities like skiing, meditation or wellness stays
- **Home stays or B&Bs** - Bed and breakfasts can be hosted/catered or independent stays and non-catered
- **Farm stays or station stays** - where cottages, shepherd's huts and shearers quarters are converted into character heritage accommodation
- **Unique and bespoke options** - like hiking shelters, huts, treehouses, off-grid pods, safari tents, converted shipping containers, and underground caves.

How to attract accommodation bookings

Here are eight ways:

1. **Target niches** - these are bushwalking groups, girlfriends on a hen weekend, 4WD clubs, school groups, networking groups, Lions, Probus, and more – in fact, any formal or informal collective that may use social media (see Facebook Groups), or groups you may be a part of that you can target online, in a newsletter, or make a presentation to
2. **Use a distribution platform** - we covered this earlier in more detail, and these include pay to play and free to list (but pay through commission) arrangements with companies like Airbnb, Bookings.com, Trip Advisor, Rezdy, or a pay to play each month regardless channel manager like CloudBedz or Guesty - just to name a few.
3. **Harness social media** - to target groups (see niches), and present your offer in different lights, keeping audiences up to date with specials, offers, news, upgrades, what funny thing your dog is doing right now
4. **Install bright and welcoming signage** at the entrance or en route to reflect the brand and experience at your accommodation
5. **List on ATDW** so you come up in searches
6. **Ensure your website is search engine optimised** for the kind of keyword searches your target markets use
7. **Package** with a tour operator or a restaurant or an event in your town or region
8. **Storytelling** - communicate your story, the personality behind the logo, the reasons you love the region in your social media, images, art work, styling selections, welcoming messages, and post-booking confirmation

Tours

Tour products include the hosted and self-guided varieties

- **Bus and coach** - short or multi-day, taking in a region or several states
- **Charter** - where more often a wealthy client is looking for an experienced driver/guide in a private vehicle to show them around, often arranged through an agent
- **Cultural** - groups or catered for the individual, hosted in a cultural context or by the leader/ guide, such as in Indigenous communities, or during an Indian festival or French Language School
- **4WD** - with a tour guide or host or tag along, and can also be self-guided
- **Walking** - walking in hosted groups with a guide/camp cook, or self-guided
- **Novel** - Scenic flights, camel treks, steam train rides, Mail Run, Outback Pub Tours, volunteering, Cowgirl for a Day, novel and bespoke experiences from day trips to multi-night safaris
- **Food and wine** - walking tours of markets, cooking schools or classes, wine and cheese sampling, degustation, or progressive dinners, paddock to plate, visiting regional farms and forests for foraging speciality produce such as truffles in regional WA, cherries in the Huon Valley, or native Australian bush foods like quandongs in Quorn
- **Educational** - Cooking, yoga, dance, art, and language schools - guests may stay on the premises, or attend during the day and stay elsewhere at night
- **Health and wellness** - this is a growing and profitable segment globally, and many regions lend themselves to wellness and spa experiences by virtue of proximity to nature. It includes therapies and experiences such as massages and spa, meditation retreats, cleansing and rehabilitation, forest bathing, experiencing nature, supervised micro-dosing, medical tourism and more. Wellness has a wide definition and wide appeal

There's a whole bunch of tours and experiences offered on forums like ATDW, and that can inspire you as to what people offer, and what people like to do when visiting your region. Many follow their special interests, so go with that if you want to share a secret skill or love.

How to attract bookings

Here are five ways to attract tour bookings:

1. **Distribute online where successful accommodation is** - try to catch their markets either at or after the time of booking online. A good way to do this is to use the same booking channel, like Rezdy, Trip Advisor, or Bookings.com. Airbnb now sells experiences, not just accommodation, and opportunities to book tours on Airbnb come up on the app or website, once accommodation is in the shopping cart
2. **Visitor Information Centres** - are often managed by Councils, and some use Rezdy or another company called V3, depending on how serious they are about being a wholesaler of tours and experiences. Many VICs just use a listing by ATDW (mentioned in earlier chapters), and leave it for customers to book direct, or call ahead, and take a fee from the operator. As a tour operator, you need to look at a number of options
3. **In-lobby or in-room promotion** - focusing on accommodation providers is a great way to sell tours direct to their customers, especially if you offer a small booking commission to the hotel for onselling to their guests. Ask to put some quality fliers in their reception or in-room compendium. Normally tours and experiences are the third thing a person has booked after transport and a bed, so your digital brand proximity (and to a degree physical proximity) to car hire, train or bus bookings, petrol stations, and accommodation will be a factor in increasing recognition of your tour and selling it (or you can package with the accommodation provider and sell a combo before people arrive)
4. **Pitch to the bigger fish** - What does this mean? Think about large coach companies such as APT Touring or AAT Kings. Well, accommodation and tours are often packaged together for the coach markets, which are always on the lookout for new ideas for their itineraries. As a tour operator, if you've developed something simple, fun and appealing to a coach company's target market (for over 70s, for example, a bush BBQ with native foods, wine and music by a campfire with story-telling is a wonderful night out), they may include it in their brochure as a fixed part of an itinerary, and pay you per person to supply it on fixed dates through the season (yes, please). You might offer the tour or the accommodation, and the company packages them up at a retail rate to offer a complete itinerary
5. **Use promo codes and special offers** - This helps with conversion for a customer who is unsure, or on a budget, and you can use it strategically to fill seats mid-week or in the off-season. Like this, you can increase bookings on slow days as well as maximising them without dropping profit margins

Attractions

Attractions can include:

National parks, wetlands, and UNESCO World Heritage areas

Community assets - swimming pools and sports grounds

Heritage sites and places of interest - physical, natural, social

Amusement parks

Cultural centres

Places like the Big Banana

Farms, cattle stations, wineries and agri-based tourism

Zoos, including animal petting

Art galleries

Neighbourhoods markets and community events

Museums and collections, folk museums

Festivals, religious celebrations and events

Shopping centres or retail precincts

Bars, pubs and clubs

Restaurants, cafés and speciality food outlets

Attractions in regions are often building based – brick-and-mortar cultural centres like VICs to help people stop, rest, and plan on long road journeys. While initially attractive, over time many – if not most – are rarely profitable and barely break even, which becomes tiring for local elected members once the original group moves on, and the investment case becomes an issue.

Bricks-and-mortar can work, but to be viable regional tourism attractions require really smart practical design (try finding and changing a specialist lightbulb in outback NT for a 20-foot ceiling!), foot traffic, an ongoing budget for maintenance, and multiple services under one roof to deliver efficiently.

It also helps if it's close to the town centre, unless you provide transport. Other free things like adventure playgrounds can keep the kids happy and, if there's good coffee or a bar, the parents too.

New buildings are a great cause of celebration and interest in a region, and their appeal to visitors should not be underestimated. A new bespoke built attraction can cost anywhere from $2m to $8m, depending on design and architect fees. But it's the daily operating costs that grind owners down over time. Once the novelty has worn off, a publicly funded attraction in a building can become a community and public burden - a white elephant in the wilderness - and there are a lot of bones in that graveyard across regional Australia.

Locals may resent having their rates and taxes put into something that is in decline, or at the end of its life. If there is not a viable business case, then really it requires courage to upgrade, reimagine, or dismantle it so everyone can move on, and invest in other things that matter more to locals and provide a return.

Take this into account if you are thinking about starting a regional attraction such as a small art gallery and workshop in a disused building. Also consider installing solar panels, cool building technology, and water tanks as a way of reducing bills from the start; the cost will be covered in three to five years, or less given our rising energy prices and the plentiful sun and wind in Australia.

Attractions - Quick Math

One of the things I get asked often is how much an average cultural centre or attraction costs to run. It's a fair enough question given the money spent on them, but it depends on the size, floor space, services offered, and average number of visitors expected. It's good to explore the average costs of things as that reveals what needs to be paid for - but then how are you going to sell enough tickets? It assumes there's a building and some staff who need to be there to greet and manage bookings.

An average attraction like a cultural centre funded by a Council or a small folk gallery or museum in regional Australia costs around $100,000-150,000 just to keep the doors open. A typical annual budget for a small to medium-sized regional attraction looks something like this - and this is generous:

Rent	$25,000
Gas/power/ Wi-Fi	$8,000
Wages (full-time manager)	$80,000
Super/WorkCover	$8,000
Marketing	$5,000
Public insurance	$1,500
Building repairs	$3,000
Office sundry, IT	$2,000
TOTAL EXPENSES	$132,500

Rent and wages are the highest costs, followed by outgoings. So to make money you need to be generating say double what it costs to run from customer bookings, let's say $265,000. Your marketing budget, location, and opening hours will be critical.

If your entrance ticket is $10, and typically entrance fees are low because the experience is often not curated very well, you need to sell to 20,000 visitors a year to make $200,000. This is hard going, because the price indicates value, and $10 we know buys you a world of entertainment over a whole month on Netflix. This is how people think.

Or you can up your price to $25, and make sure it's a great experience, and then you only have to sell to 9,000 people.

How to get bookings

The quickest way to do this? Here are 10 ways to attract bookings :

1. **Be relevant to your target market** - and aim to be among the top three things to do in your town/region
2. **Make the core experience as appealing as you can on your budget** - or apply for a grant to invest in professional layout, visitor flow, sound, lighting, storytelling, branding design and marketing
3. **Have consistent opening hours** - even when it is so slow that your cat walks out bored, stay open
4. **Engage a curator** - or someone with a flair for theatre and drama and interior design
5. **Have signage** - or, if you are on a budget, a well-designed sandwich board and flags - all the indicators on the street that you are open for business
6. **Offer group discounts** - attract groups of people, and encourage locals to sell you too
7. **Give locals an incentive to come by** - offer free entry, and encourage people to bring visiting friends and family
8. **Partner and package** - with local accommodation and restaurants for a great day out. Include morning tea in the price. Try things out to get people in
9. **Stay open** - during events, weekends, festivals, market days. Crowds create interest, which then creates crowds. Humans have FOMO - fear of missing out - more than we like to admit
10. **Create something curious** - our curiosity sometimes gets the better of us, and that's when you can make money.

Just to put this in perspective, MONA and Luna Park charge $30 per person entry, and their operating budgets and capital expenses are much higher than $130,000 a year. They get say 300,000 visitors a year. 300,000 at $30 each is $9m in revenue a year. Not bad. Not great if your operating bill is $8.75m, but still. MONA does this in lots of ways, and invested a huge amount early in the building, the grounds, fighting Councils, and the curation of artworks and customer marketing and engagement. It grew over time. They created some curious things like their Dark MOFO Festival to extend Tasmania's summer season into winter, built accommodation for people to stay on-site, and provided the MONA Roma and MONA Ferry from Hobart to transfer people from town to the museum with a drink as they take in the beauty of the Derwent River sitting on a hot pink pig. They change exhibits regularly so there's a reason to return, and it's a solid fun day out, love it or hate it - they sort of like it if you hate it. All their marketing is fun, trippy, and has an attitude that is distinctly MONA.

People do love it or hate it, but at least they feel something, and many go out of sheer curiosity. Check it out when you can.

What is an experience?

The experience gives the emotional impact a visitor wants when they book a holiday. Experiences can be positive, or negative if things don't hit the mark, or in the case of MONA, just so outrageous that they leave some people frothing at the mouth while others are stunned or delighted. This is an authentic experience too.

Travellers may hear about a spooky restaurant and want to have the bejesus scared out of them while demolishing a medium-rare steak. Many people enjoy the mild anxiety of being locked in a themed Escape Room or being the smarty-pants who can solve the riddle with their friends and escape. Some love the feeling of being immersed in nature and being in their body, swimming in gorges, kayaking on rivers, lazing on beaches, going on a yoga or dance retreat. Many people travel to pursue a personal interest more deeply: a friend of mine goes to jazz festivals all over the world, my mum flies to Paris each year to go to language school, and I'm a mad Writer's Week tragic - some go for photography, surfing big breaks, or smashing out new downhill single tracks. Travel is a time to cultivate, explore, and develop an unattended part of our psyche that doesn't get much attention during our normal working family routines and commitments.

People are quirky - that's one thing you learn in tourism. Everyone has their thing, and as a tourism operator my view is that our job is to indulge people, let them do their thing, and make them a surprising offer to experience something new, or something else. Let them revel in whatever it is they want, provide them with the options and information and a landing pad, and, voilà, your job is done. It's no surprise that people are easy to please when they are doing what they like. Their biggest decision, to be there at all, has already been made. But to get the booking you need to sell the experience people can have at your place.

Regional experiences

Experiences lie in regions and destinations as well as in activities, and knowing what your region's core experience is will help you to sell your own tour, accommodation or attraction. For example, the Gold Coast conjures up mental images of miles and miles of surf, tall buildings, hibiscus, and rich, tanned blonde ladies with little fluffy dogs. If I say Colorado, you may think of mountain ranges, skiing, and horse ranches and American cowboys. If you say northern India, I think rickshaws, bright saris, tea stations, and wicked hot beef vindaloo. This is how our brains work - association creates emotional impressions and meaning, shortcutting our thinking pathways for us.

Tourism destination marketing, as I have covered, relies on visitors knowing these codes in visual communication. It can also work in the negative. If I say Warsaw, you may think cabbage rolls and snow. If you say Rio de Janeiro, I may think crowded slums, and street kids. I'm not saying this is accurate or right, it's just how our brains associate with media portrayals and stories over time, unless we have more intricate first-hand knowledge and know the stories behind the images. Their tourism commissions may have some work to do to get us there.

Curating experiences - the Five Es

A little bit theatre and a little bit psychology, curating a visitor experience means using creative tactics, identifying the key stories, themes, and activities tourists will be invited to take part in. Many people have travelled widely before coming to your region, so are quite sophisticated experience seekers. You need to find a way to reveal something about your town or region for them to feel they are learning something new about the place. There are many ways to do this. With the senses:

- **Sound** - music, atmosphere, silence, bird song
- **Lighting** - artistic, directional and functional, lighting building frontages, light show projections onto town silos or old buildings
- **Tactile** - food and plants tours, a national park, bark crunching underfoot, bedlinen and crockery
- **Smells** - like campfire or the food guests are about to eat, the saltbush in the garden
- **Sight** - sculptures, landscaped gardens, entrance gates, fabrics and interior design.

Five Es of a compelling customer experience is another framework that you can use. There are variations of this around, but over the last decade working with regional tourism managers I developed this process as Clear Vision Consulting's own tool to help operators to step through their place or town and do a self-check audit to see how the visitor would experience it. The stages are:

1. **Entrance** - What is the entrance experience and its physical location - is it easy to find, or a secret access point? How will someone know they've arrived, and how can I make them feel welcome? What is the first impression I want them to have?
2. **Engagement** - What are the mechanisms to engage guests in my business or purpose? Is there quality tea and coffee when they arrive? Or a concierge to take their bags at the spa? Can guests sit and play instruments or music in the B&B, and is there interesting artwork on the walls? Or secret spaces in the garden to explore? Can I capture their attention with the lights going down in the gallery before the show, or do I want them to engage in their own time and way?
3. **Excitement** - Will people talk about this experience for a long time? Have I raised their heartbeat in any way? Have they seen/done/learned what they came here for? When?
4. **Emotion** - Do they want to leave a different person to when they arrived? Do they know more about themselves, this place, the people who live here, when they drive away?
5. **Exit** - As they drive away, do they feel good about having spent their money here? How were they treated? What will they tell their friends?

Sectors

Tourism sectors include market and industry - it's a way of differentiating who we are talking about at a time, given the industry can seem wide and deep and complex. Examples of sectors are:

- Accommodation
- Tours and transport
- Hospitality, restaurants, pubs, clubs, event venues
- Museums and cultural tourism
- Regional tourism
- Festivals and events

Many of these sectors are characterised by their own peak bodies, and are often responsible for standards, have members, and work with them on best practise and overcoming red tape. Some are unionised and even have their own super funds, but mostly when a tourism person talks sectors they are referring to what part of the industry is being affected by an issue or event.

Niches

Niches exist within markets and destinations, and if you have a special interest you may find others do too and will travel to pursue it.

Kangaroo Island is among other things famous for its pristine beaches and native honey. It is home to endangered Ligurian honey bees brought from Italy a century ago. The Island's tourism operators have been exploiting this niche for years - Italian honeymooners love the idea of a beach-based holiday in the south of Australia, and more so because Italian travel agents can sell a connection to Liguria, giving their markets a reason to choose South Australia over the Whitsundays.

Melbourne is a UNESCO-listed International City of Music. A jazz bar in North Brunswick works with a local boutique hotel to package show tickets and accommodation to jazz lovers travelling globally to hear their favourite musicians play.

An Indigenous community just outside a national park has built a lodge nearby to accommodate large groups. Private school and education groups and volunteers visit to help work on the lodge and learn about Indigenous culture by spending time with community members formally and informally.

These examples demonstrate niche markets where, if you can tap into them and if they are deep enough to sustain you, you can do very well with a focused marketing strategy. Now that's super geeky marketing stuff right there.

Destinations, products and experiences are ultimately the structure of regional tourism - the skeleton that shapes it. If your destination does not have certain products or experiences that a target market would like, then this is an opportunity for a new business or idea like yours.

Let's summarise

- Destinations can be countries, cities, regions, also businesses or attractions
- Destinations can be designed with consideration of the Five As - Accommodation, Attractions, Activities, Amenities and Access for different visitor markets
- Products are attractions, tours, accommodation and experiences. They can also be transport, food, events, and other tourism or travel services
- Experiences should resonate with positive aspects of a visitors' emotional state, and can also be communicated in regional and destination branding
- Five Es of an experience are Entrance, Engagement, Excitement, Emotion and Exit
- There are six key sectors in the tourism industry
- If you are in a crowded market, you can do very well by specialising in a niche market using a focused marketing strategy

Killara Distillery Richmond, Southern Tasmania. Moon Cheese Studio

CHAPTER SEVEN

Regional Characteristics

REGIONAL REALITY CHECK

The next step is understanding what is really going on in your region.

Do you live in the place where you sell your experience, or live in another town and manage it remotely?

What makes regions loved by some and scorned by others?

What are the challenges and barriers that you may have to overcome as a new regional tourism operator?

Try this exercise:

Recall an overseas trip. Do your memories involve being outside a city in a National Park, or in a village having a deep, meaningful conversation with a local in their home – perhaps in a language you don't know, but somehow you understand? You may remember the local café in the square, a small restaurant, sunrises, the night swims, the long treks? Chances are you were not in a city.

Post-COVID, now many of us are working from home or spending more time working on the road thanks to more flexible working hours and mastering online meetings. At the beginning of this massive shift in how Aussies work, thousands of people vacated major cities on the east coast for more affordable and attractive lifestyles in regions. For some, it meant buying property, but others took to the road and started blogging about #vanlife on Instagram.

What did they blog about?

Well, many were suddenly shocked by regional reality as they grappled with the good, the bad, and the downright annoying.

In Australia, no two regions are the same, and all regions are not equal, so there are some things you should be aware of before you set up or buy a regional business. If you are new to regional Australia, then you or your guests and staff, may be in for a shock.

Some regional realities

- **Some regions have terrible water.** Many inland and outback towns rely on bore or ground water. You may have to change from mains to rainwater tanks when water is low, and talk your staff or guests through it

- **Many regions still experience Wi-Fi black spots,** meaning terrible mobile reception or no way to get mobile reception or enough signal for Netflix, online games, Facebook, Insta, let alone emergency warnings from the Country Fire Service, SES or updates about cancelled flights. You will need to warn guests about this one

- **Australian regions are often very remote and have extreme climates** that can change departure times, dates, opening hours and physical access. They are susceptible to floods, fires, droughts, and plagues of the mice, mosquito, and locust varieties, wind, snow, humidity, sandstorms, and blazing sun. I won't even mention the critters

- **The cost of living is often more expensive than in cities,** even though the rent or mortgages may be cheaper. If you are in a small town of say 2,000 people, there's probably less competition for tradespeople so they may charge more per hour and per kilometre. Costs include travel, and booking can take weeks or months

- **Access to fresh fruit and vegetables** is not always as reliable as in cities if there's no farmers' market or if towns are not near a Coles, Woolworths, IGA, Aldi or wholesale delivery

- **Many regions' young people leave** - often having been educated in cities where they meet friends, marry and stay, so playgrounds for kids and activities for young adults may be limited in a town with an ageing population

- **It is harder getting access to quality professional and medical support** - many towns don't have a bank branch, local hospital or GP, accountant, or lawyer, and even if they do there is not always the variety or choice in businesses and services

- **The workforce in small regional towns may be scarce** - or unskilled, or people may not value local work. They may be skilled and prefer to work in the mines and make 50 times what the hospitality industry offers. Tourism competes with agriculture and the resources sector for workers in hospitality, trades and maintenance

- **The customer service may be better** - but possibly worse if people are uneducated, lack travel experience, racist or simply not interested in out-of-towners

- **Locals may simply distrust out-of-towners as meddling** - and undermine your investment if you haven't done your homework or put strategies and relationships in place

Despite all this, or possibly because of it, my message is: don't give up. You can still be successful in regional tourism. Creativity loves constraint, so it's time to get creative.

As a regional tourism business owner you will, more likely than not, grapple with some or many of these barriers. Here are some strategies you might use:

- **Be prepared to pay more** for maintenance, labour, cleaners and gardeners. This means you need to build in a good margin, which you are likely to need to maintain vehicles, buildings and inventory

- **How you handle and communicate with your customers matters.** It sets the tone of their adventure and expectations with advance advice and warnings. Remember, no one likes surprises

- **Within reason, you can sometimes make quirky things work in your favour** as part of the experience. For example, rainwater and native gardens will appeal to ecologically minded visitors. Low or no Wi-Fi will appeal to people looking to unplug

- **Invest in local relationships early.** If you are new to a place, it helps to work out who has influence, and who is likely to support you - or not. You may be upsetting the apple cart unintentionally, so talking to a range of people, and watching how the town divides - normally who drinks at what pub - is a good insight. Introduce yourself to the local Council or Progress Association, and let them know who you are and what you are doing. You don't need to pick a side - try and get along in a small town

Regional characteristics matter

All regions are not the same, which is a paradox for regional tourism - we love diversity as consumers, but as operators and marketers it would be easier if we could just copy what works in other successful regions. Some regions on the west coast, such as Bunbury Geographe, have major regional centres, shopping malls, airports, thriving mixed industries other than tourism, and are within an hour's drive of a capital city. This presents different challenges and problems to say, Northern Rivers NSW or Mt Isa QLD. Even within states, regions are radically different. Just think of the destination brand of the south coast NSW region compared to the outback like Broken Hill - not just their geography and climate, but their politics, the social demographic, and business types and sizes. Regions are not one homogenous group, and it's essential to understand the nature of your region as this will help you work out what challenges you may need to overcome locally to attract more bookings from the exclusive niche markets that you may want to tap into.

How can I determine my region's characteristics?

You may know your region like the back of your hand. Or you may be buying or building a property or starting a business in an unfamiliar town. Either way, seeing things from an outsider's point of view helps when you are planning the tourism experience. A good place to learn about your region's characteristics is a website like Regional Development Australia (www.rda.gov.au), which publishes statistics on the population, key industries, and major projects in the pipeline that can alter tourism attractiveness, especially if a new airport or train link, or a major hotel or visitor attraction like a new World Heritage listing is on the cards in the near future. These things attract people and interest.

- **Look at the voter base in the town.** Is it a working class or a more well-heeled electorate? What about the shops along the main street. Are they well-known brands? At the high or the low end of spend? Make no mistake, property developers and retailers do their homework on the local demographic before they invest in an outlet. So if there are a lot of Cheap as Chips and Bargain Basements, and Country Road has moved out of town, then it's an indicator that times are tough for locals, and the discretionary spend has evaporated or moved elsewhere - online probably. This is for information only, but will affect your base of employees if you need staff, and also the perception of the town

- **Work out where or if you can get support locally by doing your homework.** Look at who is on your local Council. Do they really support tourism, and is that form of support tangible for you as a business owner, or just lip service? If you have a local tourism organisation (LTO) in your region, or an RTO, do their committees reflect a diverse community, all genders, and from a range of cultures, ages and industries? In many cases, decision-makers on Council or community tourism and business committees do not reflect the diversity that's in town or on its way, which may mean you will have to work harder to innovate, get support, or persuade decision-makers if they don't share your or your customers' vision and values

- **Look at who's advertising in the regional paper** if your town has one, and who is investing in promotions in the regional community. Search Trip Advisor and see what the Top 10 things to do in your region are, and how the town is rated by visitors. Are there any obvious gaps? Is there something missing you can offer that no one else is doing or selling? It might not even be that crazy – just something very simple, an add-on to things people are already doing. Perhaps a bus transfer at the end of a three-day hike, or a picnic lunch for a business market travelling somewhere remote for work

How regions are packaged with cities

As discussed, most regions attract an intrastate market – that is Victorians travelling around Victoria, Queenslanders in Queensland, etc. Recent research has shown that regional experiences are often added to a visit to a capital city, either an interstate market flying or driving into a main airport or town, and then out for a few nights in a wine region, hiking area, or a natural seasonal event, or a regional intrastate visitor visiting the CBD for shopping or a family event and then going on to another region they always wanted to visit. Whatever the market, the principle is that capital cities feature for a large percentage of visitors, so it's worth considering if you should be doing some marketing in these cities to influence decision-making.

If you are a micro or small business, this is impossibly expensive, but here are some ways, especially for an attraction or tour as these are often booked at the last minute. Any additional exposure of your brand can reinforce your name, location, and experience for a visitor.

- **Package a regional tour or experience with accommodation in a city**, and sell through a domestic wholesale distributor. Distributors include Qantas Holidays, Rezdy, Travelpoint, Great Aussie Holidays, and the NRMA. This is quite a sophisticated strategy as it often means working with an agent or a wholesaler as well as having a good relationship with city-based accommodation marketing managers, and splitting costs and sharing customers. Domestic wholesaling is quite a big topic, and a next level strategy you can read more about in the Resources section at the back of this book and online at my website under Booked Out Resources (www.cvconsult.com.au/bookedout-resources). There's a great information sheet called Packaging, wholesaling and commissions by Business Victoria

- **Quality coloured flyers and postcards are popular in brochure racks** in city hotels, hostels, and major attractions like museums and galleries. This may be a bit old school, but it is repeat brand exposure that boosts your visibility in a market looking for things to do. The closer to your region these fliers are, the more targeted you are

- **Network with the city-based Visitor Information Centre** who still use such racks mentioned above. The 55+ market (Boomers) and some internationals do frequent Visitor Centres. Having your brochure there and meeting the staff to update them on your accommodation or tour is a good idea when you're in the city

- **Seek an opportunity to sponsor a physical banner, or public signage at an event or sports club.** If you are linked to an event, sport or type of experience, consider channels or places that people gravitate towards, and negotiate a sponsorship if this is your target market. You might pay an annual fee to the local netball club to have your business brand on the court or uniforms or, if you have a restaurant in a wine region, you might fly banners at the farmers' market next to a food stall

- **Advertise in the printed regional visitor guides** often distributed in city hotels and motels. People take them on the road, and flick through to do their research

Regional branding - how does it work and why should you care?

Chapter 3 provided an overview of how regional tourism marketing connects to state, national and international marketing, marketing structures and how to use them, and who is responsible for promoting what. In Chapter 6, we covered what a destination is, how destinations are linked to products and experiences, and how this is used by RTOs and STOs to promote certain destinations to target markets. Now let's look at what you can do in your regions and business to bring your brand to life, and the impact this can have on bookings.

Regional branding is a way to categorise, and help consumers to understand a region's strengths and plan holidays better. Many people, once they have decided on the state they are going to, use the WA Tourism or SA Tourism site (whichever STO) to create their own itinerary, selecting from available products and experiences (drawn down from ATDW mentioned in Chapter 4, a very helpful tool for planning). If your product isn't listed on the STO website, chances are you won't make the itinerary of the people who use it to plan and book. This collection of experiences starts to build a picture of the regional offer and brand. Is it gourmet, outdoorsy, fashionable, high energy, cosy or something else?

How to use a business brand to stand out in your region

Brands tell stories about a place or an experience - they do this through colour, word use, placement with images, typeface - a whole other world (and book). It's amazing just how susceptible we all are to brands. We love them as brands make it easy for us to categorise quickly, make decisions, and align our values and needs with the product options we are comparing. We are wired to connect, to tell stories, and to relate socially. So if you have time, I suggest you play with a brand name for your business - give your boat or house, or top-selling tour a catchy name, something fun and memorable. People love it, it sticks, and it allows easy recall - which you want if people are going to refer to you or come back and book. They're going to remember Flipper's Fabulous Dolphin Tours.

Another tactic that works in branding is creating cognitive dissonance to get people to pause and look again. This is when opposites coexist, and jar our brain to take note by messing with the meaning. For example, I call my B&B The Outback Shack. Shack sounds a bit shabby, but when they see the reviews are 4-5 stars, and that I charge a reasonable amount - more than a shack, but not as much as a 4-star hotel room - suddenly there's curiosity and name recall. I also tell a different story to my competitors: one of calm and serenity. Come and look around, hang out in the garden is pretty much my message. Being memorable and easy to recall is what a brand is for, and doing it on a shoestring with good story-telling and a catchy name is even better.

Design in your brand communication also signals quality, and the experience people can have with you. It's especially good when your design and interior styling reference the local region, heritage, quirky stories, interesting characters, what the rooms were used for in the past, and which industries were in your street. Gawler Ranges Safaris in Eyre Peninsula SA do this really well in their safari tent styling, with local woods, fabrics, and art featuring the local critters, plants, and wildlife. A lot of properties can start to look the same. We all read the same interior design magazines, so there's no unique brand anymore. Do something quality but different that describes your building, town, local characters of yesteryear. Stand out for something - create curiosity.

For and against regional tourism brands

Within the state brand are a subset of brands. The regional brands. These matter - and don't. This sounds contradictory but I'll give you the for and against, and you can make up your own mind about regional branding, and if or how it helps your tourism business:

For

- Regional tourism brands are supported by the Tourism Commission, and reflect the region's personality
- Branding gives industry a shared identity to get behind
- Brands should reflect shared values and experiences, and develop trust, which helps operators to pass business around to one another
- A regional brand can cut through the noise of how a region is seen and understood by those outside it, such as federal funders or new investors. Cut-through is essential in a noisy market, especially when there are 77 tourism regions, seven state brands, and hundreds of Shire and Council brands vying for attention
- A regional brand is a quick way for travel agents and third parties to understand the kind of experience on offer, and if it's aligned to customers' values or interests
- A brand saves time and attracts the right sort of customer

Against

- There are 77 regional brands. How many can you name?
- Research shows that despite millions spent on regional brands, rebranding, logos and print, there is still low recognition of what to do in regions from target markets interstate. That's Aussies not knowing what they can do in other states - and they live in the same country and may even have visited that state before
- With all the layers of branding at state, region, Council and business level, that's a lot of visual messaging to get through if you are a consumer, and a lot of points where people get distracted and wonder off. Oh, look at that shiny thing...
- Most people travel for personal interests or for work, which dictate where they're going anyway, so do regional brands even matter? Won't people just research, and book when they get there and work it out?
- Many consumers use big aggregate online guides like TripAdvisor, Google Reviews, Booking.com, or Airbnb to get their regional information about what to do and where to go, so really does a region's brand even feature or add value in the consumer's decision-making and booking cycle?
- The further away from a region you are, the less familiar a regional brand is - the logo, colours, icons and typeface may not resonate without local cultural cues

Regional Grants

When you are small, you are flying solo. Should economic troubles hit, as they do every few years, and markets suddenly bottom out, grant programs pop up to support industry, but the reality is that little is aimed at small regional tourism operators and you should not rely on them as a way to get started or pay for capital.

> **Tip:** It's a better strategy to have a profitable business and save a buffer in the good times so you can diversify and survive when things get tough – as they invariably will. If you have money that can be matched with a grant in hard times, you are in a good position to invest in your future, and create scale or competitive advantage.

Being able to tap into state and national regional tourism grants is a big step, and by building a buffer and focusing on profits, you put yourself in a good position to take it in year two or three with some runs on the board.

Grants are a way for a government to get operators to spend their own capital (grants often require a matched amount from the operator) as well to move cash into the economy, especially in the last five years as the value of the visitor economy and dispersal into regions has been widely recognised among economists, government and Council CEOs. Grants have become a way of driving capital project planning and spending readiness. These large grants are great for established businesses with a good business plan, site surveys, and Council approval, who were perhaps going to spend anyway; there are few tourism operators who have a lazy $20,000 and more to invest.

There are also other types of rural and agricultural grants that become available through RDA Boards, history and heritage bodies, and if you have the time to manage them they can be an excellent source of capital for a project that would not otherwise go ahead. Grants are great for collaboration between operators to bring about new trail infrastructure, or fund a feasibility study in a region, or branded signage, or an app that links social histories to a free town tour and keeps visitors longer.

My view is, there are probably easier ways to make money than relying on grants. They have their place, but some of the downsides include:

- Many grants are aimed at a narrow group to achieve the funders' aims, not the business's, and you can spend a long time trying to be a round peg in a square hole

- Grants take an enormous amount of time to apply for, and in the early days this is probably time you can spend working smarter and getting the fundamentals bedded down
- If successful, you need to acquit them and also pay tax on them
- Sometimes the money arrives late as governments are not the most efficient organizations, and stall over paperwork. This has upset some businesses I know, which committed to a project and then had to take out loans to get a working capital extension to pay trade contractors until the funder released the grant. It created a lot of unnecessary stress and unplanned interest fees and cost

Beware the offer that sounds too good to be true

Outside of STOs, federal departments and agencies also invest in tourism and offer grant programs throughout the year for business planning, marketing, infrastructure, interpretation, product development and feasibility studies, each with their own criteria and focus. But be careful to read the detail before getting excited about finally putting your big plans in place. The devil is in the detail, and sometimes the initial offer sounds too good to be true, because it is, for most commercial organisations and SMEs with small budgets. If you are a Council, an Association or an Indigenous organisation with resources, some of these grants may suit you better. These include:

- The National Indigenous Australians Agency (NIAA)
- The Federal Department for Regional Development - (the old Building Better Regions Fund or an iteration of this going forward)
- Natural Resource Management Boards (NRM)
- Primary Industries in each state
- Others.

TOURISM BUSINESS PLANNING 101

Quantifying regional market size

If you do go for a grant, you will need to make a business case, and part of this is knowing your region's market size. As you move from start-up to growing your business, or if you are already on a farm and diversifying, or have an asset and are adding a tourism experience onto it, like a cellar door or a cultural museum, knowing your market size will help you:

- Work out your business's market size
- Set bookings targets
- Work out your likely occupancy
- Be confident you can get a return on your investment, because there are enough people to book
- Apply for a grant (or loan from the bank), and show your bookings estimates are not pie in the sky, but based on facts

> **Tip:** Knowing your market potential versus how many people you actually need to make a profit are two different numbers.

If you ask a tourism operator how big their target market is, most will quote you the historical number of total visitors to their region in the Regional Profiles by TRA. This is not wrong - it's a great stick in the sand - but not all those people are necessarily interested in that operator's product.

For a more accurate reading of your region's tourism potential, look at all the emerging niche markets, and how many of them are around Australia.

For example, the number of people interested in 4WD tracks in the outback, are likely to be the population of all the 4WD Clubs and Associations in Australia, plus a percentage of people not in clubs - say international visitors plus their partners or friends, and possibly a handful of grey nomads and some international students out for the trip of a lifetime. That number - and you'd need to do some desktop searching to estimate it - is your regional market size if you are selling an outback 4WD tour or experience, or running accommodation on a remote station.

So when I estimate a target market for clients, I don't just look at the TRA Regional Profiles, but specifically who else may come with some more target marketing. I want to know how many more of the potentials my client can convert within their available occupancy and resources. That is target marketing, and it relies on identifying niches and researching them to come up with a reasonable estimate.

How to estimate your tourism business's market size

Above, we covered quantifying your region's market size. Now we look at your business specifically.

The regional size or number is probably bigger than you'd actually need to make a margin if you just had one or two tour vehicles, or a 12-bed accommodation facility. If you are developing a targeted bookings plan, or a business case, you should know your business capacity and your target occupancy - how many people you can service at one time before the profit drops off. This is limited by your seats, standing-room or bed capacity, so you have to know:

- Are there enough people interested in your product in your region to get a good level of bookings?
- What does your revenue looks like at a particular occupancy?

Many niche markets are not tracked by STOs unless they have a dedicated resource to do so, so you will need to go digging - or pay a consultant like me to do it for you. Some other places you can use to estimate your region's market size are Caravan Park Industry Associations, the local VIC, or road data counters by National Parks or the Department of Infrastructure and Roads if they publish them. Also, try universities or education peak bodies who publish international student numbers, or any peak body for the niche groups you want to attract - say photography or mountain bike clubs. Sometimes the peaks will publish how many members they have, and some of these will be your target market. Convention Centres plan for meetings and incentive conferences and events (MICE) in advance, and report on delegates coming into larger regional centres.

Once you have collected the estimated regional market size of niche groups, estimate how much your business needs to attract to get to 60% occupancy of your total capacity. It may only be 3 or 4% of the total niches identified, or more in a small region. So if you capture 3% of the target market of total visitors, what does that look like in dollars? How much would each person spend, and what would it cost you to service them? Do you need to capture more or less of the market to make a reasonable profit? These are questions a good business planner will answer with business modelling, and something you can come to my business to get tailored help with.

Tip: It's a myth that you need to have the majority market share to be profitable or successful. But what you do need is to hit your occupancy sweet spot to maximise your earnings and profits at whatever size or scale your business is.

What is my occupancy sweet spot?

Many people assume more is good, but sometimes it is not. More is often more to manage, and sometimes above a certain sweet spot more costs more, eliminating any gains. So 100% occupancy is a sign you need to raise your prices or consider scaling - or both - fast.

This can be difficult to demonstrate to lenders and funders, but it is your business and only you can persuade someone why going for 60% occupancy is more sustainable than 100%, and why you need a 12-seater sooner and not a six-seater to meet the identified future demand.

For every business, there is a sweet spot before profit declines at a particular occupancy. It's often around the 60% occupancy mark in accommodation, depending on the business model, operating costs and market variables. Anything over your occupancy sweet spot creates more maintenance costs, more wages, and higher bills, and this starts to erode profit margins. That is why charging more when you are busy is not mercenary; it's sometimes necessary to cover the cost of being full all the time, and standards and reviews possibly dropping because you can't get in there to fix things.

So how can you tell what your occupancy is?

Here's how to work out your occupancy as a percentage for accommodation in a given period, say a day, month or year.

$$\left(\frac{\text{Number of rooms occupied in a week}}{\text{Total number of rooms available for sale}}\right) \times 100 = \text{occupancy percentage}$$

Then you get a percentage, and that's your occupancy rate. You can substitute rooms for seats on a tour, or maximum entry numbers into an attraction.

At any occupancy level you will have certain costs, so keep track of when your expenses are rising sharply - often it correlates to an increase in bookings over a certain point. If you can get those costs down and maintain your margin you are doing well, but often this is not the case. Extra costs come with extra demand and use.

Tip: These added costs are called step costs - when costs rise significantly at certain levels in business operations to meet growth in demand. It's an accounting term, and a cost that good managers track to make sure you get the most out of the extra you are paying, and maximise your returns.

Find your occupancy sweet spot, and try to maintain it throughout the year. This, of course, means you need to know your numbers, and track them regularly. Occupancy worksheets can be created or downloaded, or your accountant may provide models.

Successful businesses must have a margin - which is the difference between the price per head paid and the cost per passenger, because this is the money that pays for overheads and then, lastly, your time.

If this is blowing your mind, you can use a worksheet on my Resources webpage, or engage a specialist like myself or a cost accountant to work through the costs and variables with you.

Your occupancy sweet spot will be unique to your business, depending on your costs and efficiencies. The devil is in the details.

For example: A simple half-day bus tour costs you $275 for a guide and fuel and snacks to leave the yard. You need three bookings at $100 to break even. But your bus can take 10, so bookings over three or $300 are needed because then you are covering your operational costs, including, hopefully, your wages. Anything over say five or six bookings is better because then you are making a profit. But below three you are losing money, so you need minimum numbers. However, at the nine or ten bookings, or 100% occupancy mark, even though you make $900-1,000 you need two guides, more food, and more stops to pick up and drop off. So more fuel, costs, and wages. You may end up only taking home the same $400 profit that you could have made with six or seven bookings.

Using occupancy to plan for growth

Another way to determine market size for your business is to use occupancy per tour or bed to work out how many bookings you need to sell to maximise your earnings and fill seats. As we've covered, your occupancy sweet spot number is useful as 100% occupancy is not necessarily maximum profit.

In a year - or 40 weeks give or take holidays and seasons - your sweet spot may be 60% occupancy, which is equivalent to getting 640 bookings as per below:

Tour A :

4 tours a week @ 60% (or 4 seats in a 7-seater) @ 40 weeks = 640 seats

Note: 100% occupancy is 1,120 seats filled.

For example: Your region has 55,000 interstate visitors a year. You decide to target 10% of this segment, or 5,500 people each year. To do that you need to sell 458 seats a month (5,500 divided by 12) or 106 seats a week, or 15 seats a day.

Then you consider your capacity to attract those bookings and fill those seats.

Your five-seater 4WD is not going to cut it unless you run it four times a day, which is unlikely. You may decide you will eventually need to buy a second car or a 16-seater vehicle to supply this demand, and start marketing to book seats out and pay off the loans.

If you plan this way, it gives you an idea of what capturing 10% of the market might mean in terms of what tours you design, how many staff you need, and what you need your marketing to achieve - what good looks like.

Now you are driving performance, not just growing organically as many regional operators do.

And of course, if you don't want to scale, then perhaps you should set your sights on 3% or 5% of the market - whatever you can manage with your existing car or capital - and that will be your peak profit earnings.

By the way, if you had 10% of the market and sold a tour at $90 per person including lunch, your average annual earnings with this market share would be $90 x 5,500 = $495,000 which is more than enough to pay off a bus loan and employ a few tour guides, and a marketing role to help you scale and sell.

Running a regional business remotely

Tourism does not have to be a full-time gig. You don't even need to be onsite or live close by to run a regional business. I've been running my accommodation business, The Outback Shack, remotely since 2015. The less I'm there, the more bookings I seem to get, and for some years now the business has not relied on my being there. If you are wondering what this takes, here are my secret weapons for remote operations:

- **An awesome sidekick in the region.** A trustworthy and capable person is essential to lean on to clean, pick up on maintenance, and stock up on consumables like toilet paper, cooking oil, and firewood. My cleaner is my right-hand woman. She lives locally, and can also troubleshoot if someone locks themselves out, or there's a booking mix-up

Tip: A good cleaner in an accommodation business is gold. Hold on to them and look after them. They cost $30-40 an hour as subcontractors, and often clean multiple properties to make a living, which is good as they are already trained, bring their own cleaning kit, know how to clean properly, and do it fast. Some may offer to do laundry too if you don't have a commercial linen hire business or laundry in your town - and many towns don't.

- **Simple booking and communication systems that you can share with your team or helpers.** Invest in these early, whether you design one yourself, pay to use a third party's platform, or integrate something off the shelf with your website's 'Book Now' button. If you systemise everything else - welcome message, directions, entrance hours, check in/out process, departure times, inclusions - your staff only needs the minimum information to do the job

- **Technology and one touch record keeping.** You want to tap as few buttons as possible to keep guests and staff informed. Mobile phone apps that make it easy to run a small business remotely, like Xero, Airbnb, Trip Advisor, Calendy, Email, Google Lists or whatever else you use, are now available for the major software programs. This technology saves time, is easy to file logically saving space and money, and means more time to focus on quality communication with guests and the rest of your life!

> **Tip:** Text based messaging with clients means you have things in writing and can refer back to issues and requests. Also, you can respond when it suits you. You can also flick a text to a staff member to handle something in your absence, although it is often better in a crisis to call. This is one of the reasons I prefer online bookings to phone bookings as it's more security, less time and less risk for me.

- **Be available with the right attitude.** You may be absent physically, but you are still the boss. The buck stops with you, and you are responsible for what happens on everybody's watch. Inconvenient things can and will happen: bookings get muddled, something breaks, staff don't show, and people dispute your refund policy. In my experience, as long as you remain calm and committed to resolving issues guests are quite forgiving if your team has dropped the ball, and can accept bad news if there's an explanation, an apology, and clear options to resolve issues in a positive, professional manner

Staff hacks for regional workforce challenges

- **Avoid sharing your staff around** as they are your secret weapon. In a region, you can compete based on your workforce, so treat them well

- **Always be on the lookout for good staff,** and multi-skill them too, even if you have a full card. Not having a Plan B in case of sickness, relocation or retiring staff, can end a good run - fast

- **Consider staff in other destinations** looking for seasonal work, such as resort staff in the tropics who may want to do a wet season down south in the dry summer, and make a direct approach before their season ends

- **Can you offer staff accommodation?** Affordable rent is a major barrier in many Australian regions, so if you can offer a studio or simple accommodation, you may get the best of a willing bunch

- **Cross-train your staff, so they are not just the** waitress, but also the pilot, cook, housekeeper and tour guide. Everyone needs to be hands-on-deck in a successful regional tourism business

- **Create function checklists for each role,** and take your staff through them to ensure that they understand what has to happen, in what order, and why. Check how they are doing on a regular basis, what feedback they have, and what they've received – good and not so good. Training and supporting your staff is not a one off set and forget - it's ongoing

- **If you have great staff, give them responsibility** so you can step away, take a break, or perhaps even manage the business at arm's length from elsewhere

- **Use shared systems like group chats, access to calendars and reservation systems,** Quick Replies for messages, cheat sheets, and task checklists so staff can manage without you there, and you can tell whom you can trust to follow instructions

INDIGENOUS TOURISM

Regions offer incredible opportunities for visitors and operators to connect with Indigenous people and have powerful conversations and experiences to help reconciliation and healing. There continues to be strong interest in Australian Indigenous culture from internationals, and increasingly Australians want to learn more directly from and with Indigenous guides, Elders and business owners. Indigenous tourism includes passive experiences like visiting art galleries, watching cultural performances, tours, and immersive events offered by Indigenous and non-Indigenous companies. I think we are missing out on a lot by focusing only on experiences and not on who owns them and where the money flows. Research by IBA has shown many passive Indigenous tourism experiences, like looking at Indigenous art in galleries, because not many galleries are owned by Indigenous people or collectives, capital city galleries give very little to no direct economic benefit to Indigenous people. However they do offer high exposure to a large number of visitors.

Times are changing, and Indigenous people are becoming more empowered and, rightly, starting businesses and owning their own narratives and stories, not just in tourism but all sectors. Interest in connecting with and learning about Indigenous culture is growing, but also problematic as it is really asking some of the least resourced people in our society to be responsible for explaining or managing the potential to respond to questions about the impacts of complex and deep trauma not of their own doing. Be mindful of this if you are planning on working with your Indigenous community as they may not have capacity although they may be very interested, and there are now many wonderful Indigenous-owned tourism businesses showcasing their culture, and skillfully managing conversations about our shared past.

Just be sure to work with a legitimate Indigenous-owned and operated business where you can, and make sure you are not being hoodwinked by non-Indigenous businesses posing as Indigenous as this may become fraught. You can check out credentials and a registered list on the Supply Nation website of all certified and registered Indigenous-owned businesses (IOBs) in Australia, although not all of them are listed here as it's a rapidly growing sector. You can employ Indigenous people or support the community by referring your customers to Indigenous-owned tours and cultural centres if there are any nearby.

What is an Indigenous tourism business?

When we talk about Indigenous tourism, most people reflect what they see, not what's possible. There are not usually many - or any - Indigenous people or investors informing these conversations. The tourism sector is very behind. We think of cultural tours, bush tucker tours, artists, and talks at cultural centres or on country. Or dance troupes performing in hotel chains and resorts as entertainment. Increasingly, there are immersive cultural experiences like my client Ngaran Ngaran on the NSW south coast, and Juan Walker from Walkabout Cultural Adventures based in Kuku Yalanji country in Far North Queensland. We don't generally think enough about Indigenous corporations owning hotels, buses and fleets of vehicles or facility maintenance companies for hotels and resorts. Or, as one of my clients dreamed and not unrealistically, an Indigenous pilot training school in the outback - but it's only a matter of time.

Definition of an Indigenous-owned business (IOB)

The definition in Australia is that Indigenous businesses are majority owned and operated by Indigenous people - that is 51% or more at the ownership level (director, management and shareholders). This is to ensure that decisions are made by Indigenous people, and profits go back to Indigenous people and communities. Research has shown Indigenous people are more likely to employ other Indigenous people and, like all of us, spend first on their own families, mortgages and bills. Also, you can't be what you can't see, so role modelling plays a huge part in intergenerational change and creating pathways out of poverty.

Looking at tourism, you can see the supply chain opportunities for IOBs in large resorts, airlines, and transport companies are enormous, not just to provide cultural experiences, but a full range of trades, services, and products.

I work with many Indigenous entrepreneurs and corporations planning to enter the industry and navigate the regional tourism landscape. Here are some frequently asked questions about Indigenous tourism:

Do I need to be Indigenous to run an Indigenous tour?

If you want to be respected, and if you respect the right of Indigenous people to speak for themselves and their own experience, then yes. But it depends.

If you are not Indigenous, or Indigenous but not from the country where the tour is, it's generally considered offensive to speak for the traditional local people or make money from posing as an authority on their culture.

There are exceptions though. Cultural tours are run by businesses that are not Indigenous-owned because of high demand in some places. For example, some National Parks engage Indigenous guides who are from the land where the Park is situated as staff or subcontractors to run tours. Yulara Resort at Uluru Kata Tjuta National Park in the NT is a jointly managed park with traditional owners. Indigenous guides from Queensland have been employed to run tours in the Park for many complex reasons, and will often protect themselves by qualifying where they are from and talking in general terms. Having an Indigenous person is better than a non-Indigenous person, but having local Indigenous people is ideal as it role models what's possible, and money flows back into families and communities from local wages. Sadly, this is not always possible, and depends where the community is at and if workers are culturally safe and supported at work.

Can I call my tour Indigenous or authentic if I have an Indigenous person on my payroll?

The word authentic is problematic, and overused in the tourism industry, all the more so when talking about who is authentically Indigenous. If you are an operator and employ Indigenous people with cultural authority for the purpose of engaging with your guests on a tour on that land explicitly understood to be about learning about culture or place or an Indigenous world view, then yes, you can probably call it an authentic Indigenous experience or tour.

But be careful not to overstep or assume. Just because you have Indigenous staff doesn't mean they can speak about culture. They are generally in a better position to non-Indigenous people, but speaking about culture in a second or third language to a sometimes inappropriate tourist group is not easy! Also, tour guiding and cultural knowledge sharing require the individual to be culturally safe, and authorised to share cultural information. They may not want to, or be able to, or be allowed to. Also, Indigenous staff on the payroll may be working behind the scenes with no cultural aspect at all. Guides may not be talking about culture - they may just be driving people from the hotel to the airport, or doing the cooking.

Is that an authentic cultural engagement? Don't overstate it if it's not real.

Gecko Canoeing and Trekking is a great business in Katherine, NT, where traditional owners are sometimes employed to guide a 5-day walking tour on the Jatbula Trail, a traditional route taken by Jawoyn people over the centuries. Mick, the business owner, has Jawoyn Rangers on the payroll, and they walk and camp alongside tourists, sharing knowledge about plants, animals, weather, language, and probably a lot of footy chat too. Mick is non-Indigenous, but he is certainly offering an authentic experience, and has worked with the traditional owners for years to build trust and respect. It's a start, and great exposure to the tourism industry for local Jawoyn in a supported way. Ideally they'd have their own business, but in this case, they are not there yet. It's just where the IOB sector is in its evolution.

Many non-Indigenous owners of a tourism business might think about leaving or selling in the future but most Indigenous people will not want to leave their place, so there are opportunities to create succession planning for the community's future and economy through tourism. If you are considering a partnership with Indigenous communities, build in training for the long term so people can learn business skills in administration, management, and finances so they can take over the business or mentor others to create their own. Sadly, there are businesses who enter joint ventures with Indigenous communities and do not invest in giving people the skills to be able to run it and take over like they promised.

How do I consult with Indigenous people?

This is tricky because while Indigenous people want to be consulted, they are also the most over-consulted and researched people in Australia, causing exhaustion and frustration about not being heard. So it depends what you want to consult about. Is it really necessary? Is it something legal, meaningful, going to bring benefit or significant impact to the Indigenous community? Put it in writing, and address it to the relevant peak Indigenous body in the specific region. Ask around. Often the cultural networks are stronger than any online listing of board members. Roles don't mean much - it is about who is the cultural Elder, the Aunty or Uncle in the community - they make the final calls. Follow up with phone calls and emails. It's the best you can do if you don't have a connection in that community.

Keep in mind, Indigenous leaders are busy, and in demand. They often volunteer on boards and committees, or could be advising the government about significant programs touching many people's lives or presiding over cultural business in health, disability, juvenile justice, and prison systems. They are dealing with a lot of heavy stuff. You are probably not going to be their priority unless you are a serious investor or they are in a position to think about collaborating in tourism.

Best practice is relationship building over time by contacting either the local Indigenous Corporation or Association. Sometimes it's a Land Council. Find them through the Office of the Registrar for Indigenous Corporations (ORIC). Write to them, make time to meet, sit down with interested people. Attend NAIDOC and Reconciliation events, show support, solidarity and connection. Be authentic yourself. Find out who has authority and who the Elders are, the Aunties and Uncles who have seniority and respect in the community.

Get to the point in simple language about what you want, be patient, and go from there.

Can I get an Indigenous grant?

If you identify and can prove you are an Indigenous person or business, then yes, if you are eligible for all the other criteria too. Check the grant guidelines that specify who is eligible.

I'm an Indigenous business, where can I get help?

If you are Indigenous and run a regional tourism business, having a majority-owned business is the first step to opening up more opportunities. This is 51% ownership to the Indigenous parties at the director, shareholder and/or management levels. It will help you tap into support at state and federal levels under the Indigenous Procurement Policies, Indigenous Business Australia, National Indigenous Australians Agency, and in some cases the Indigenous Land and Sea Corporation, which really prefer to work with Indigenous Corporations and landholders, and not only on traditional lands. Each state also has a range of IOB support programs, and most STOs now have a dedicated Indigenous Tourism Officer. NSW, QLD, WA and SA have had dedicated Indigenous tourism operator associations in place.

Indigenous souvenirs

If you are thinking about selling Indigenous branded souvenirs in your tourism business, and you are buying them online from a supplier who claims to be authentic, a word of warning: do your homework.

Most Indigenous souvenirs in Australia (those dot-painted pine boomerangs with emu footprints in hot pink) are made in China or Indonesia, but sold as authentic and locally made. It's an unethical mega multimillion-dollar industry run by phoenix companies on the east coast who never seem to quite go away, despite numerous investigations and news reports, and you'd be best not to support it. You can avoid it by purchasing gifts and goods from genuine Indigenous artists. Find them through regional art centres, and buy goods like scarves and punu (wooden carvings) direct from official Indigenous art centres. There are many, and you can get list of authentic art centres in Central Australia - Desart just for starters. Look for the equivalent in your state by attending Indigenous Art Fairs, and talking to art centre managers across Australia. You will also find some fantastic Indigenous suppliers on creative ecommerce platforms like Etsy Australia, which specialises in handmade and vintage crafts that may better reflect your destination and brand. Designs may show local flowers, animals, and references your guests can understand. Be prepared to pay more as often there are not the economies of scale behind Indigenous makers in Australia, which means regular supply can become an issue. Still, it's good to start somewhere.

Let's summarise

- Regions are not all the same, and each region faces different challenges
- Determine regional characteristics by demographic information and data on RDA websites
- Tapping into regional branding can help you align your tourism business with what the region is known for
- There are pros and cons of regional tourism brands, but done well, brands can cut through marketing noise, and help people to recall and find your business
- Regional tourism grants are commonly available, and can help if you have funds to spend, but also have downsides, and are costly to apply, manage and acquit
- Finding your market size and occupancy sweet spot are next level concepts, but can help you to make the business case needed for large capital grants
- It's not appropriate to tell Indigenous cultural stories or history without permission, training, involvement, and approval from Indigenous people or Elders
- Whether a tourism business is really Indigenous or not comes down to the ownership model, but if it's 51% Indigenous-owned and operated, then it's an IOB, according to Supply Nation's definition
- Know where your souvenirs come from. For ethical and sustainable sourcing of Indigenous souvenirs, contact Indigenous-run art centres and makers from your region or state

Juan Walker, Walkabout Cultural Adventures, Kuku Yalanji country Far North Queensland

CHAPTER EIGHT

Becoming an Operator

Congratulations. You have acquired or established a new regional tourism business, have an ACN or an ABN, and are now a member of the local tourism body or Council and ready to invite all the tourists in. Tick, tick, tick. You are officially an operator – woohoo. Let's go!

Crickets.

You have gone through the checklist provided in this book or downloaded from some other site. It should read something like this:

- Get a website
- List on ATDW
- Sign up to a tourism industry association
- Design a logo
- Attend a conference
- Take four photos of people having a good time at your business
- Open an Instagram account

These are all important parts of your new business. But something is missing - and it's a big thing.

What you need are enquiries – leads – *bookings!* You may have had a few customers, and you're super excited about these... but not enough are converting into actual paying guests. After a few months of occasional visitors and a few tyre kickers, the bills start to stack up, and your business/life partner is suggesting a part-time job might be a smart move.

So then you wonder, what else do I need to do to make this happen?

You think privately, hey this tourism thing is not that straightforward. I'd better work out how to get some control here, or you shirk it and fold, sometimes blaming everyone else for not supporting you. If you've read this book, you know I have pointed out that the reality in regions is that you are a long way away from official support, and will have to support yourself until you are sustainable and successful enough to attract official attention.

Twelve to eighteen months in is when you start to put on 'big girl/big boy pants' and really show up. You've been through one season and had some bites, but you need more. This is make or break time.

Is your regional tourism venture a hobby or a business?

How seriously do you want to build a business?

How much do you really want this?

What is the cost of failure: personal, emotional, financial, social?

Will you look back with regret if you don't give this everything you've got?

At this point, even if you have asked for support or help you hear crickets. Crickets chirping in the night and no bookings are every entrepreneur's greatest fear, but in most businesses there are waves of quiet and noise. Some people nail it and have great bookings from day one, but most don't.

Either way, here are some questions I am frequently asked.

FAQS FOR START-UPS

Is there a grant for start-ups?

The short answer is, no, not for start-ups, and there are a few reasons for this. Grants are usually taxpayers' money, and half of all new businesses fold in the first two years. It's high risk for the government to invest without any track record or evidence of feasibility. If your business requires a lot of equipment or a special building design, you need to plan to be able to afford to get established, and have some capital to invest.

Later, after 18-24 months, stage two may involve grants, but generally not in the first 12 months of your operation. Investors and government support businesses when they see a sustainable, profitable venture that the owners are running according to plan. You need to demonstrate viability, commitment, and early success, and that only comes with experience.

You need to be able to show the following as a bare minimum:

- Forward and past booking records
- Financial statements showing cashflow
- Market demand evidence
- Consistent service experience
- A three year business plan

And preferably a profit so you can co-contribute to your project as many grants require this so risk is shared.

Who can help me?

That depends on what kind of help you need. There are four main options:

1. Start up hubs or co-working spaces

There are start-up business hubsin many states now, where free or inexpensive hot desks are available with workshops and peer-to-peer networking. Unfortunately, few of these are regional, and not many are industry specific, but see if you can join digitally, or if there's one in your region.

2. Regional or local tourism bodies

Your regional or local tourism industry association is the best place to go for workshops and networking and skills workshops online. Tourism Commissions have fact sheets, great consumer research, and strategies available on their websites so you can see the big picture, but don't be too literal about what support is available for you in these documents as they are not always implemented as promised.

3. Regional Development Australia

Regional Development Australia or RDAs can be good sources of high-level economic development help, demographic information on major projects, population statistics, grants, and business advice of the generic kind, and sometimes have Tourism Development staff who can give you broad information, from networking to conferences and skills workshops. There are 53 of these boards across regional Australia, so certainly one can help you.

4. Large global tourism businesses

Large global tourism businesses have great resources, public research and reports, blogs, cheat sheets, and how-to guides. I use them often to reinforce basic steps, and I pick up news and insights all the time. These include Skift, Deloitte Access, Caravan and Camping Industry, Google Travel, and more. They have Community Forums, short blogs, newsletters, and lots of information online as they have become experts supporting their members and customers. Signing up to newsletters (you can always unsubscribe later) is a good way to learn and get across skills, trends, and news - if you have the time!

Why doesn't the Tourism Commission feature me in their campaigns?

I've worked with some angry, vocal operators in the tourism sector, disappointed they are not being helped or promoted as they expected. The STOs do cop a lot of this fire, and it is frustrating to be met with silence or indifference from a government department not knowing how to engage with regional communities. Often the loudest people care the most, but still, the reality is there are limitations in the sector.

If when starting out - the first two to three years - you are promoted over and above your own efforts, my advice is to consider it a blessing, not a right and definitely not an expectation. In most states there are hundreds of small regional tourism operators, so it is unreasonable to think all or even half could be featured in state-wide promotions, Awards nights or grant programs, no matter how deserving we think we are. My message is you can be small, profitable and excellent at what you do, even if the STO is not actively promoting you in campaigns or PR or familiarizations. They need established, reliable operators with experience in domestic and export markets before they take the risk of recommending you to their contacts.

You need to forge your own path, and grow before they pick you up. If you make yourself known to key people, network, and get scale so you can increase your staff, turnover and bookings, then the STO is going to take notice and consider you for their trade and consumer promotions. Be specific about what help you want – there are many things STOs can do, like introduce you to networks and agents, support grant applications, and refer you when you aren't there, bringing many valuable contracts and business. So be careful before you criticise too loudly.

What are entrepreneurial behaviours?

Some of the key ideas here are behaviours exhibited by successful entrepreneurs and tourism operators - and it's not necessarily what you might think success looks like. These include:

- Being prepared to back yourself and take a risk
- Having a clear vision about what you love about your region and your business purpose
- Not being pretentious, just comfortable with reality as a conservative starting point
- Learning how the seasonal waves play out
- Developing local partnerships
- Sticking it out and finding better ways
- Paying it forward
- Paying yourself last
- Paying your tax and bills on time
- Building and keeping value in the business and on the balance sheet
- Understanding and admitting your weaknesses
- Sharing business referrals around
- Employing, communicating expectations to, and coaching other people
- Hunger for knowledge and continual improvement
- Reinvesting in what makes money
- Being able to recharge and take a holiday regularly
- Looking after your own mental and physical health to go the distance

When you are truly hustling and doing all these things, doing what it takes to keep your business open and afloat, and then growing the heck out of it when you can, then you are effectively an operator.

The Tourism Operator Journey

Understanding yourself, and not just the mechanics of the industry, is a vital part of growth in becoming a business owner and a tourism operator. Of course you don't have to play any game, but if you want to become a successful operator not just a hobbyist, it starts with self-management and understanding the situation you are about to embark on. There are predictable stages, trials, frustrations and lessons that regional tourism operators face. We've covered a few: learning the language, being initiated into regional realities and terminology, the challenges of finding good professional support, feeling overwhelmed, early success, working the government marketing levels, and developing new digital marketing skills.

As I drive around, I enjoy listening to podcasts, such as Dent, and She's on the Money, and also to the stories, trials and tribulations of entrepreneurs - the heroes of their own epic journeys. Some of the obstacles people overcome are phenomenal - with a great deal of luck and risk involved. You too are on your own heroic business journey - and it really is epic!

The heroic journey is a concept coined by Joseph Campbell and adapted by Hollywood screenwriter and script adviser Christopher Vogler. Vogler reviewed ancient Greek myths and legends, and hundreds of scripts to see what made a story more believable, and why some films resonate with audiences more strongly than others. He found the films that worked better all had the main character or hero going through a major personality transition. Your journey to becoming a successful and established tourism operator is not dissimilar. You will come to see that the tests and barriers you face are predictable; you can become familiar with them before you set out so they are less threatening, and you can see things for what they are, and overcome them sooner. Importantly, you want to reach the end of your journey! Understanding common pitfalls and stages can help ensure that you don't settle for a premature end, or fall for false limits.

Borrowing Vogler's structure the regional tourism operator journey goes something like this:

Ordinary world

You are doing your day job, minding your own business, dreaming of maybe one day starting a tourism business, or perhaps just wanting a tree change where you can relate to the people around you better, and do the things you love.

Call to adventure

Someone dies and leaves you a house, a business, a small fortune. You get fired. Your husband leaves you. You see an ad in the paper or a friend tells you about a business opportunity not far from you. You need to make some money. Why not? What have you got to lose? All the kids are grown up now...

Refusal of the call

Self-doubt emerges. Your family look at you like you're crazy. Your ex says it is just another phase, and your friends say that would be a nice little hobby, meaning you can't be serious! Your dog is the only one that wags his tail. He's in!

Meeting with the mentor

You call your old boss, who has spent her whole life following her own interests, runs a successful company, and still makes plans for her future. You meet a woman on the bus who runs a marketing department, and she gives you her card. You get talking to an architect who tells you about the countless business plans he's seen that wildly underestimate the return on investment timeframe for a new build in the region. Your yoga teacher tells you your spine strength will help in all areas of your life - and suddenly you get what he means.

Crossing the first threshold

You sign the lease, buy the business, quit your job, get the loan. You make appointments with architects, wrestle with website designers, buy the land. You step out and sign up with the industry body. You leave the naysayers behind.

Tests, allies, enemies

You clash with Council rules on outdoor dining, and discover plumbing leaks, but track down a helpful local tradesperson. The bank won't refinance, your graphic designer goes on strike, and you can't find the staff you want. You meet local business people, share issues and build networks to find a new team.

Approach the innermost cave

Bookings start to come in - your finances are on a thin edge, and your stress levels keep you awake at night, but you feel alive! You have committed everything and so far it's working, although you are not paying yourself and your veggie patch is neglected. That rustic country garden just isn't a priority. Your marketing is humming. Bookings are good, you employ staff, and contract some part-time help in the office.

Resurrection

You find new markets and are more able to capture market share with less effort. Your business goes from strength to strength. You can get a loan. It is easier to attract skilled staff. Backpackers stay and work in the region, providing a much needed workforce for other industries. You employ a manager, and step out for a well-earned break.

Return with the elixir

You have built something with its own brand and legs, and new businesses have popped up around it. A new market is coming to town thanks to Council investment in bike trails, local industry is humming, and the town wins awards. You are helping other operators in your role as chair of the regional tourism board, where you can use your experience to guide others. You sell the business to a buyer who pays a great price, and you leave the industry.

Or not.

The road back

Council gives you a reprieve on rates for a year. You apply for and win a grant. Your business partner invests so you can add more rooms, a kitchen, upgrade your vehicles, and extend marketing. You wholesale with a tour company from the east coast, and secure bookings 12 months in advance.

Reward

People remember you stuck it out with them and are loyal to your business. You meet a like-minded business partner who invests in you. You are featured in a travel magazine for attracting a fleet of food vans, turning temporary housing into quirky eco shelters for backpackers, and creating a unique destination that people are flocking to. You are shortlisted for a regional community award.

The ordeal

There's a baggage handlers strike, airline cyberattack, a flood, and an economic crisis. People stay at home - and lose their homes. You have a fire in the kitchen. It's hard to find staff. You have to reach deeper, re-mortgage your house, rebuild, and find new customers. You decide to outsource food and build eco shelters for the local community to use while waiting for repairs.

Signs you are an operator

Becoming an operator is an outlook and an evolution - fast for some, slower for others. Language does matter if you want to be taken seriously in business, so while you may feel a bit strange referring to yourself as an operator, when things get serious that's exactly how you will be seen - as the business owner who is committed and has ridden a few waves and is, mostly, in control of their boat in all kinds of seas.

My rule of thumb is you are an operator when your tourism business is more than a side hustle. Many people get into tourism accidentally, then find it grows beyond their expectations - this happens more often than you'd think, so be careful what you wish for, and be aware of your motivation and your exit plan.

You have moved from hobbyist to operator when you:

- are making income from selling a service or experience you can claim on your income tax return to the Australian Tax Office. If you make more than $75,000, you register for GST and Pay As You Go (PAYG) each quarter
- meet fire safety and Council by-laws, comply when asked to open your business for inspection, and are told which improvements are necessary
- have to represent your business publicly in your town, in your region, in your state, and in your country. You may need to work at many levels, manage relationships carefully, and collaborate with other operators whom you may or may not particularly like. You share similar customers, so collectively you are attracting people to your town/region for the greater good. These are your colleagues in regional tourism, and it helps to get to know some of them, so go to the occasional AGM or Christmas Show
- ask your accountant to set up a separate set of books for the tourism entity as a stand-alone business so you can track financial performance
- employ staff, or contract help to deliver an experience. And these people are essential - without them you would not have a business, so you need to negotiate pay, and manage contracts, performance and quality. You must have difficult conversations if the cleaning is not right or a guest loses something valuable on your cleaners' watch
- ensure a safe holiday and work environment for guests and staff, and have all the right insurances up to date in case of a natural disaster or other problems
- are thinking about upgrading your furniture, paint job, outdoor settings, and booking desk, but trying to work out how much is too much to invest to make a return without being stingy
- answer the phone and call people back, or explain how to book over and over again, and still get a kick out of someone doing your tour! Making money doing what you love never gets boring
- call yourself an operator when you introduce yourself to someone at a function or party
- are proficient at Xero, can create professional presentations for agents on Canva graphic design software, organise your social media posts on HootSuite or Meta, and update your own website and blog like an influencer

Yep. These are all signs that you have moved into the realm of being an operator. Check you out, superstar!

Systems that sustain your business

Checklists work, but they are not the work

I'm a list writer, and a big fan of getting things done, but checklists never seem to end, and if you don't get away from the day-to-day to look up and set some direction, it's easy to think the checklists are the work. They help - don't get me wrong - but they are not the work. Filling in a checklist is not the work. You did everything they told you? But were you paying attention? Did you follow your gut instinct? Did you come up with some of your own ideas? Solve some of your own problems? When you started on the checklist, did you come up with a lot of other questions that needed answering? I bet!

While well-meaning, many advisors are not experienced, and don't take the risks they are asking you to take, so their attitude is that 'doing tourism' can be summed up in a simple checklist. They may believe it - you may believe it - but don't fall for it. Completing tasks on a list is not the same as getting your hands dirty, and developing perseverance, patience, insight and your own discernment.

For example, at the top of one of my checklists in this book is get a website. In reality, when you have spent $5,000, money that was going towards your mortgage, or kids' education, and months with a graphic designer fighting for every detail on your website (after ticking off YouTube marketing videos on that check list), you know in every bone in your body that website needs to start generating bookings, pronto. Accreditation will not help this. Doing another course will not help. You must get out and start winning contracts, sending traffic to the website, having meetings and getting bookings. You have to be grounded in the basics and get things done, and keep doing them until they are a habit.

Now that should be on a checklist!

A Business Plan is essential

Regional tourism businesses generally don't make healthy profits or a decent salary for their owners without scale. Before you start up, think about getting scale if you want to leave your day job and make enough revenue to support yourself and the business as well as staff. To get scale you need capital to expand, to buy a new vehicle, build new rooms or a new reception area. When money is cheap and interest rates are low, it's a good time to borrow if you can repay. A lender will want a business plan to demonstrate how these reimbursements will be made, how you will address risks, the strength of visitor demand (see the section on how to estimate your market size), and how you will attract your target markets. This is the work I do day in and out with clients.

As a professional adviser, I see a lot of business plans, but most are 'hope plans'. Typically, these are vague numbers not supported by any facts or competitor research. Business owners can see the opportunities and risks clearly, but are normally too close to the everyday to acknowledge blind spots or the risk of thin markets and to ask the tough questions. To have the courage to assess performance in a small business is rare. Generally this happens when people are at a crossroads, up against the wall, losing money, getting ready to grow and seeking investment, or wish to sell. Before you forge ahead, it is essential to take stock, see what has been gained, and what else can be done to boost productivity before you invest in a venture whose foundations are weak. Get tourism fundamentals strong and keep them strong, and the rest will follow.

Most business plans are execution documents - especially at start-up, when there are hundreds of tasks and things to do. Nothing wrong with that.

You probably only need a business plan if you are asking someone to lend you money, or have to communicate complexity to a number of people with vested interests, to show the business case and due diligence in a transparent, factual manner. The riskier the venture feels, the more a business plan can help you iron out weaknesses and threats, and address them with new strategies.

A good business plan should answer hundreds of questions - hard questions - and save you time explaining everything all over again when you are busy. It shows the bank you have done analysis, and the facts and figures of the market opportunity, and your role. These questions are: Who is the market? How will we compete? What are industry benchmarks? What is our mission? What will we charge? How many years will we operate for before we reinvest or sell... and on it goes.

A bank lending money will want to see financial projections to know their loan will be repaid. So yes, a business plan is a must for seeking loans, grants, engaging with your staff and business partner, articulating strategy - how you will get from here to where you want to be in five years.

Underperformance

While it's great to make money, because the businesses in the industry tend to be small there is massive under-performance in the sector overall. What do I mean by this? A good business should sustain the owners and pay its own way. It needs to do more than break even. My definition of a performing business is one that generates enough value for customers to be profitable and grow in size, what it offers and/or revenue, and pay its own way. What's yours?

Around 80% of the wealth would be in the top 20% of the industry, or even less. Tourism has the seriously invested, and then everyone else.

It's very similar to the agricultural industry, where I have worked as a financial counsellor to small family farmers, who may be reasonable producers (or not), but struggled to make good business decisions, and are now responsible for managing a third or fourth-generation farm they may never have wanted or dreamed of running. They've realised making big business decisions is a lot harder than it looks, having never administered a company, and never been taught by their parents, who probably didn't know either. Most of us are self-taught.

The issues are surprisingly similar: there are not always the economies of scale on small farms or tourism businesses, people are technically good at something but not necessarily great business people, and succession or exit planning in a family business is often fraught and badly handled, if at all. Many farms, like tourism businesses, exist only just making a profit and living off the business, which is not great. The assets are in the ground or the stock, and they can only make money at certain times of the year. They are hit by global economic events, petrol prices, transport costs, interest rises, and trade agreements.

Why am I talking about underperforming farmers and tourism businesses? Because there is an imperative to shine a light on what you are doing so you can run a business that is rewarding, and working for you. You need to keep your eyes on the financial ins and outs so you know how you are performing, your profit, your costs, and your game plan.

It does not take great talent or specialist skill to run a hotel, or lead a tour, or drive a car; you don't need a degree to do it. There are quite low barriers to entry in tourism. So it's easy to be in the underperforming category, and have a profile, and look successful even if you are not actually growing and strengthening your fundamentals.

If you are only breaking even in your tourism business, I urge you to really question what you are doing and why so that you do not get caught with bills that you cannot afford to pay, and a declining customer base or asset values. Is it time to sell up, move on, and cut your losses, or are you ready to bring in some help, identify weaknesses, invest in yourself, and grow?

Developing a tough skin

Addressing business performance issues requires mental toughness. But it's worth it. Firstly you've got to get that ego out of the way!

The tourism industry can be quite warm and fuzzy. Tourism people love to network, and it's easy to believe the hype about how great we are, how well it's all going, isn't it wonderful! Aren't I great? Sometimes having too much smoke blown up the proverbial can blind us to helpful, sometimes unwelcome, feedback.

Be careful not to surround yourself with people who tell you what you want to hear all the time. Everyone has their own sensitivities when it comes to taking advice and feedback. Acknowledging our weaknesses means being vulnerable before we can be powerful. Let's face it, we all have blind spots about our own capabilities, performance, skills, and behaviour. Being in business will bring these to the fore like nothing else. People give unsolicited feedback, and criticise without ever having met you, which can be hurtful and trigger self-doubt and negative thinking, or denial. You need to find ways to manage this, yet ask yourself if there was any truth in it. The best advice I can give is to foster an attitude of curiosity and openness in the early days, and ask the right people for advice, help and assistance.

The fact that you're reading this book is a great start... but it's the start not the be-all. You need to seek support and advice continually. Talk to your partner. Join a Facebook business support group. Better still, pay a coach or mentor, someone whom you trust to give you direct insights, a different point of view, to help you reframe issues so as to stay empowered with choices. It works - not only in business, but throughout your life.

In business, developing a tough skin is essential, and can take years, but it lets you keep going, and grow beyond your competitors, up to the next level.

MASTERING FUNDAMENTALS

Here's what I regard as the tourism fundamentals you need to nail down in the early and intermediate years:

The primary series (years 0-3)

1. Your website works, meaning it can be found, and people can book and pay online. If you are attracting direct bookings to your site, you have thought through what people are searching for, and the key words they use, and have your web copy search engine optimised (SEO) to rank on those searches. You have found out which reservation system works for you and any third parties who also sell you, and their systems and calendars are integrated with yours
2. You use your logo and brand consistently on email signatures, Google listing and social media
3. You are on Google Maps as a red teardrop, list as a Google Business, and actively manage your business details
4. You are in touch with your regional visitor information service - through your Council most often - and have let them know you are open for business
5. You are listed on the Australian Tourism Data Exchange (ATDW) , and update your listing annually
6. After every booking, you follow up with an email from your customer database, and send them a link to Google Reviews to leave a comment, and ask them to refer a friend
7. You use at least one third-party distribution system or referral agent such as Airbnb or Stayz if you have accommodation, or TripAdvisor and Rezdy if you are an attraction. You may also use national agents and wholesalers like NRMA, and specials like TravelAuction if you offer an experience or tour

The intermediate series (years 3-8 or earlier)

1. You set up a company ready for growth to keep from risking your personal assets
2. You employ others to manage when you can't be there
3. You cop criticism from someone in the industry, a negative online review, and you bristle with defensiveness, but suck it up and respond appropriately. You realise that five negative comments out of 100 do not dent popularity for the majority

4. You become accredited as you see the value of going for a tourism award, which will give your brand a higher profile in the state, and competitive advantage in your regions. Hey, you may even make it to the Nationals!
5. Your bookings are consistent each month, and growing, or are peaking or plateauing. Your business is divided into two key markets after a few years of experimentation
6. You consider expanding into more accommodation or adding a tour to upsell and cross-sell your original service to your current guests
7. You set bookings goals, and average occupancy, and your metrics are consistently reached
8. You are paying more tax, which means you are also earning more money
9. You engage a business adviser to review pricing, and research new markets interstate and overseas. Also to identify the best places to invest money
10. You are getting more enquiries from groups or unusual sources, possibly even third parties who like what you are offering and want to partner, or send their guests. Will you block out dates...?
11. You have experienced dry spells, and understand it's the economy not you, and you start to work with trade and enter interstate or export markets to flatten out the booking dips in your normal markets
12. You start to see all the ways you can add value and sell the heck out of it - free lunch, free firewood, free use of the sauna and jacuzzi, 20% off dinner at the local pub, we organise picnic packs, have you booked the Steam Train ride yet?
13. You start looking at taking more risks

Beware the blind mantras

There are many things wildly overestimated as necessary to run a successful regional tourism business, but that are not important to consumers.

Here's a list of some of the 'essentials' I've come across over the years that make me roll my eyes:

- **People need perfection to be happy** - Uh no, that's the control freak in you or your adviser, not your visitors
- **You must be on ATDW to get exposure** - If you are an event or attraction, then yes. But for tours and accommodation, this completely depends on your target market and distribution strategy
- **People know to go to the VIC to enquire** - If you're over 45 years old, then maybe. There are now two new generations of travellers, Gen Y and Millennials, who didn't grow up with road trips, don't know what VICs are, and if it's not on their phone or in their feed, then it's not real...
- **Being accredited will make you look more professional and get more bookings** - It will also cost time and money in the early years, and many customers don't recognise what it means
- **You need to post daily on social media to attract bookings** - Saturation turns people off; you'd be better securing group contracts or a distribution partner to ensure you hit breakeven
- **Direct bookings are better than paying commission** - Not if your distributors reach new markets that you couldn't, or if you are too time poor to service customers directly

These statements are hogwash.

Sadly, they've become mantras from industry experts who don't look at the detail or context. The truth is, it depends on your markets, on your size, on your business model... so many things.

And so much regional tourism advice is repeated without any thought of changing world circumstances, regional or local events, social media influencers, data and AI. A lot of advice remains stuck in the past, because the people giving it are - and I mean this respectfully:

- **from another era** - Until recently the consulting profession has been largely middle-aged or just plain old - white guys in suits who have come from banking, accounting or corporate advisory firms and don't get small businesses or regions, and their data and systems are not bespoke. They have fabulous data and tools, and think big when it comes to tourism, but not so much the journey of how to get there

- **reliant on data from historical research,** without regard to information from other sources such as experience, anecdote and untracked market behaviours

- **often part of or beholden to peak bodies** or agencies for their livelihood, bodies which often take credit for tourism visitor growth and expenditure correlating economic growth to marketing campaign activity when there is little evidence to support this

- **no longer growing,** researching or thinking for themselves or independently, so the way advisory is provided remains a reflection of how it's always been done, even if there's no real change or outcome

- **disrespectful of regional people,** seeing them as hicks and too far away to be a priority, and patronising without actual commitment or equality

- **from another industry** - many people come into tourism from agriculture or marketing without any background in the ins and outs of the history of the tourism industry, let alone knowledge of operations or customer service

- **plain talking shit.** There are as many tourism experts these days as there are low entry barriers. If they get out a checklist in the first meeting - red flag!

- **making it up to stay relevant.** It's easy to take what works in one industry and wrap it around onto another without regard for nuances or accuracy. Is your adviser insured and liable for their advice? If not, take your grain of salt with you

- **thinking a position or a role makes them an expert** - causing great damage and confusion

- **disrespectful of the consulting profession and of qualifications,** believing anyone can give advice, right?

- **not aware of what good looks like,** or what a business growth journey can look or feel like

- **not prepared to take any risk themselves,** despite encouraging businesses to do things they would not, or could not do

- **not accountable** for the impact of airy fairy advice

- **churning over someone else's advice** without understanding the deeper application, caveats or subtleties that make all the difference in application

- **not really sure how to harness technology** or social media, or even respond to world events in a practical sense, because they are usually on a salary so don't need to from a financial standpoint

- **resistant to deeper analysis,** reflection, feedback, and taking personal responsibility for mistakes

The list goes on.

Sometimes it is better to trust someone who says look, I don't know. Let's put it to one side and come back to it. That shows a lot of confidence, which only a competent and grounded adviser has.

If you work with government or regional tourism officials, you will hear black and white thinking, or what I call blind mantras, that includes advice such as:

- High-yield markets are better and more sustainable with less impact and more profit

- Export markets take three years to get into (some tourism businesses start with an export strategy from day one)

- Internationals spend more (mostly because they buy a long-haul plane fare and spend the rest in CBDs).

I collect these responses because they are such predictable generalisations, as though having a checklist of things makes it all simple. They say these things because it's easier for them if you comply and don't query them. I've spent a long time asking questions, learning my trade, and implementing things I've been told to do by experts, only to realise some things work, and others don't. In regional tourism, there is more going on than meets the eye, and there is more than one way to get bookings, which I hope by now you can see and start to apply in your own business or town.

Handling hard times

I believe a sign of being a successful regional tourism operator is surviving hard times. Having a financial buffer and/or a higher profile and better reputation are helpful strategies to survive longer and pick up extra business if others fold. This is yet another reason to develop a performance point of view when you start out.

We are all at the mercy of market forces. They are a part of business life. The Australian regional tourism industry has been struck by a plethora of disasters over the past 20 years - they have not let up, and include drought, flood, bushfire, disease, strikes, a high Australian dollar, the global financial crisis, volcanic ash, tsunamis, more floods, the pandemic, more bushfires, more floods. During the first two years of COVID, many tourism operators had their markets dry up overnight. Government grants helped some, but not all.

> **Tip:** One of the lessons from COVID is those businesses who had a buffer, or the ability to find new markets or scale to take more demand from impromptu markets, survived and prospered. Without a buffer, your business may struggle to ride out some of the waves the industry is notorious for.

Especially if you are small, it's good to keep this buffer intact, and reinvest in your product, marketing, and offer every couple of years - or consider what scaling might look like and if you can afford to, as scale can provide some protection and also more profit.

If you are marginal, treating your business like a hobby, and often taking money out to treat yourself, chances are you are eroding your buffer to survive the inevitable tough times.

Handling critics

Included in the toughening up theme is handling criticism.

Every successful person and business deals with this, so how you respond to it matters.

The more successful you are, the more subject to attack you will be. People project all kinds of things onto you, your business, your brand, and the perception you have created. People who don't even know you.

Let me share some of my insights:

- Tourism is about people, and reveals shitty things about human behaviour
- People lie to get a booking
- Customers have parties and damage things
- Sometimes customers don't show up at all
- You will be blamed for the weather
- You will be blamed, named and shamed for any inconvenience
- You will be negatively reviewed by people who didn't read your instructions
- People will love you until suddenly they don't
- Customers will have opinions about your cleaning standards, how comfortable the bed is, the sheets, the coffee, the way your receptionist looked at them, the overcooked eggs, the banging gate
- Customers are nice to your face, and then let rip in reviews

People love to complain; it makes them feel like an expert.

Then within the industry you'll be judged on reputation. You'll be told by funders you are not eligible for this grant or program, or sorry we already helped you once, or you don't really fit with the brand or the target market. 'You're too much' or 'you're not enough.'

My advice? Life is long and seasons are short.

If most of your customers are happy, you are on the right path. Keep going if you are enjoying it, doing what you want, and making money.

Not taking it personally, or at least being philosophical as you consider the situation, is a sign you are developing a layer of tough skin.

If we only did things that people like, and only supported things that fit into our world view of what is right, enough, or on brand, the world and travel would be very, very dull. And there wouldn't be many people travelling.

Managing people is just another part of managing business - and managing yourself as you become a fully-fledged tourism operator is a huge achievement, and shows growth and resilience.

Ways to say no without saying no

Have you ever caught yourself saying yes to something, and then grimacing when you hang up or leave the meeting because you just know that it's going to come back and bite you?

Have you said yes to be polite, liked, good, thought better of, for social currency, to fit in, or out of guilt?

Me too. It sucks.

Decide whether you want to be liked or respected

A coach I worked with used to say it's better to be respected than liked. Sometimes I've had to question this wisdom, but when you are up against it and need to take a stand, are you a people pleaser or can you show leadership even though it may not be popular? The pressure to please is enormous, especially for women: we are socialised to be nice. But you can be sidelined and miss out by being too nice.

> What would life be like if you let go of the need to be liked and did what you wanted to? What if you gave yourself that permission? Saying yes too often can take you further away from your priorities.

Busy people get stuff done, but martyrs suffer unnecessarily. Saying no is essential if you are prone to taking on too much and aspects of your business health and personal relationships are beginning to suffer.

So how do you say no without blowing it? Why is no so hard for some of us to say, and for others to hear? Saying no, the polite refusal, sets boundaries and lets people know you have been down this road before and not to waste their time. Giving your reasons with clear, polite and friendly clarity helps. People pleasers find this really hard, but it is liberating not taking on responsibility for things you can't control.

Embrace guilt and weird emotions

Developing a tough skin includes saying no more, having boundaries and backing yourself up in difficult situations. Even just trusting your own ideas about how to do something despite being told otherwise. Sometimes you have to draw a line. Or you need to commit the time to a project or pay the money. You will know you've got this right when certain calls stop, and more of the right kind of people start booking.

Raise your prices

After three years of operating the Flinders Ranges Outback Shack, I raised my prices because I no longer wanted to explain why I charged $60 for cleaning even if someone promised to wash their own dishes to get a cheaper deal. I end phone calls pretty quickly when someone is looking for a discount. You see, I started to believe in the value of what I was offering, and to defend it more fiercely.

Stop showing up

I stopped attending industry events as they added nothing to my bottom line. I cancelled my membership of industry associations for the same reason. These things don't make you money - although they can give support if you need it.

The truth is, I made more money by saying no clearly and early. My mentors and advisors told me this would happen, but I didn't believe them. They also said if I raised my prices, I would get more bookings. And that was true too.

Don't negotiate unless it's to your advantage to do so

What did I learn? I know the value of my offer. My customers know the value, and that there's a line I don't negotiate over. I guess a lot of folk must, because of the number of times people try it on. I suggest maybe they should try the caravan park in the next town. Or, they can book for next year, like my current guests did last year and are loving it right now.

Sorry, I'm booked out!

Creating fear of missing out (FOMO) is a tactic that might seem mean (yes, it is delicious), but it's necessary to retain dignity and establish boundaries. People can be assholes when they want something from you. Don't ever be desperate. Creating a sense of 'Actually, no, you are missing out', that your business is very popular and you don't need to bargain, gives you power - it has to be true though to work. I'm convinced that saying no, pushing back when appropriate, having confidence in what you are doing and why, are all a part of developing the tough skin you need to keep going and building a stable, long-lasting, successful business.

It also means you can start to trust yourself more, and tell the difference between a bullshitter and a realist, a real opportunity from an empty bookings pitch, genuine concern from a guest, or from someone who did not read the fine print and insists on blaming you. Know your rights; use the law. Wake up! Shit happens - be ready to ride it out by schooling yourself.

Enjoy your ultimate power.

Let's summarise

- There are rarely grants for start-ups in tourism. You generally need at least two years of trading before you are eligible, although if you are Indigenous there are exceptions
- The STO will help you but, in a general sense. Not until you are established with at least two to three years successful trading and some scale under your belt will they consider you for referrals or campaigns, but network with them directly anyway through your RTO/LTO
- Entrepreneurial behaviours include developing a proper business plan, understanding business performance, saving a financial buffer, watching your spending, saying no (without saying no), focusing on profits, and positioning yourself to be ready to invest when the opportunity arises
- Mastering fundamentals will set you up for success. In the first years, it's the basic channels and systems, and getting comfortable as a new operator; then it's about leveraging relationships, adding new products, and Accreditation and Awards platforms
- Handling critics is a skill you will need to learn to stay out of the emotional dramas of disputes. Criticism comes easy. Stay focused on creating value, setting up systems, and the next customer
- The Tourism Operator's Journey follows some predictable and common phases - know which one you are in to get mentally ready for it - and let me know, because I love hearing about it
- There is a lot of advice given in the tourism sector. Make sure you are getting advice from a qualified, experienced professional who is insured and accountable for the advice they provide

Wooleen Station, Murchison, Tourism Western Australia

CHAPTER NINE

Can I Really Make Money from That?

THINGS PEOPLE PAY FOR

In my first year at art school, I knocked together a bunch of wooden key holders with hooks on them from dad's shed, covered them in photocopied images of bugs, and varnished them. They looked pretty cool - no one else had a key holder like that. They sold at an art school market for $30, and I couldn't believe someone would pay me for 15 minutes of work that I enjoyed and found so easy to do.

It got me thinking about what else I could make that people would buy.

Here are some lessons based on weird-but-true traveller psychology that I've learnt over the years watching people.

People pay for space, privacy and security

Would you believe me if I told you that you can make $200 a night selling space? Not a bed, or an experience, just space. Think about it. That's all accommodation is. Four walls - sometimes not even that: a patch of grass, maybe a roof or tent, and suddenly, it's 'somewhere else'. It's pretty simple. That's the bones of it.

People buy a space to sleep and maybe shower that's yours for a short time. The more random or quirky the location, the more likely someone will want to stay in it. Sometimes people even tow space behind them all over Australia for what works out at a lot more than $200 a night. Don't underestimate the value people place on feeling secure, especially in a new region far from home.

You can make money from special knowledge, telling stories, and showing places only you have access to

People sit in the pub and tell stories for free. Many of them are full of shit, but it's still pretty entertaining. Then imagine if you actually have something to share - special knowledge? A skill or a craft? People will pay for your knowledge and time. Look at your passions and interests: making art, drawing, ancient civilizations and cultures. Dance. Spirituality. Food. What would you pay to sit with an expert in your field, and ask questions and get answers?

People pay hundreds of dollars to see spiritual leaders and high-profile authors, such as the Dalai Lama, Marianne Williamson or Eckhart Tolle, a guy who self-actualised while sitting on a park bench. They talk about concepts that are available to all of us, but 'out of reach'. Yoga teachers show us how to breathe and move better, stuff we're born doing, although granted we could all benefit from stretching more often. These teachers are normally very skilled, and communicate with impact - the good ones anyway.

People take their interests with them and will pay to learn new things from experts

If you have something special to share that is structured, good value, easy to book and pay for, and memorable for all the right reasons, people will probably be interested. So why wouldn't they also pay you, a farmer who knows how to handle animals, a winemaker with a passion for distilling gin, an Indigenous woman with stories about her ancestors and access to native plants and medicines?

People pay for you to do it instead of them

Any service you can offer, like breakfast hampers, dinners, picnics, add-on tours, laundry, transfers, specialist tours, dog daycare, pet hotels, linen hire, house cleaning, gardening and maintenance, you can make money from.

This is the age of the service industry, heralded by demographer Bernard Salt who writes entertaining and insightful demographic analysis of generations, our buying behaviours, and how we are shaped by our times. He was in part responsible for linking Gen Ys and Millennials to smashed avocado brunches for $25, while lamenting being unable to afford a deposit for a house. The growing wealth in the Boomer and middle classes has us outsourcing all the mundane things that we don't want to do and are willing to pay someone else to, so as to create more time for ourselves to do other things that make us more money, so we can pay more people (or just do other things we love).

You can make money transporting people

People need to move through space and time. Be picked up at the end of a walk and driven back to their hotel, airport, train station. Many regions don't have bus services because it's hard to get economies of scale, but perhaps you can find a way to set up a bike hire service or be the first in your town to offer an charter bus service to the trail head or rail station, or deliver local takeaways to the caravan park or B&Bs.

You can make money out of locally handmade, authentic souvenirs

Screen-printed regional flower patterns on paper or material stapled over a wooden frame sells to regional hotels as destination artwork. Then you can take the same design and put it on tea towels and T-shirts - just black ink on white fabric. You can set up an online shop and sell them direct as merchandise to people all over Australia promoting regional art or better still your own business brand for $15 or $20 each.

People pay to get back to nature

You can create reasons and opportunities for people to be outside with a small transportable fire pit and some wood. Most people don't have open fireplaces in their homes: they are expensive and messy, and kind of inefficient - not to mention not environmentally friendly if sourced inappropriately. But if you do have a good supply of sustainable firewood and a safe space to set up an open firepit, it's a simple, pretty, cheap, and effective way of getting people outside at night, and talking, looking up at the sky, gazing at stars, and working on their survival skills rather than staring at phones or the TV.

People pay to get away from it all

People will pay for solitude - simply to be alone for a short while. Many women have never had this experience, responsible for raising families and being partners, carers, workers, constantly around others, craving their own space. Writers and artists need it to create and go deep without disruption. I had a manager stay at my beachside apartment one summer to do her planning in a two day stint. She lived in the same town, but needed to get away from home-life distractions to focus on the year ahead.

Create opportunities for personal, intimate and solitary experiences. With some lamps and a table, paint, textas and paper, a bit of glitter, glue, tape and any other raw materials you have at home, you can turn a treehouse or an old garden shed into an art hut for guests to play in while they are staying on your property or campground, or visiting your attraction. The best thing is, they can make a mess. Or it could be a reading hut, or nook with a stack of books and a comfy armchair near a small window letting in light. You'd be surprised how many people are willing to dabble in a new hobby when they are out of their normal context.

These are simple concepts, and people do make money over and over again from doing simple things.

Another point on weird traveller psychology: something happens when people are on holiday. They move into a new space disconnected from their home reality where they are bombarded every day with marketing messages about what they need to feel happy and complete. Being away from all that, they are unencumbered, and it's a great feeling. In this mood, and if you target people with disposable income, they are more likely to pay for things that they might baulk at if they were at home.

This said, when people are travelling they have needs that are legitimate and real to them, and if you want to be in regional tourism there is plenty of room for you to offer a whole range of options and services, doing what you are good at, and bringing together other suggestions and services that enhance your main offering.

Yes, you can make money from that!

Let's summarise

- Create simple and affordable opportunities for people to have experiences at your place if you run accommodation, tours or attractions
- Food hampers, transport, souvenirs and merchandise, opportunities to be alone, be outside, be creative, be lost, be found, or just be still are all ways to make money
- People appreciate you thinking about their needs before they know they have them
- On holiday, people are more likely to pay someone else to cook and entertain them and to try new things
- Some people are rich. Even if you aren't, others are, so don't think about yourself on holiday, think about your ideal customer

Lake Mulwala, Mulwala. Courtesy of Destination NSW

CHAPTER TEN

Regional Tourism Business Fundamentals

Define what success means to you

Success is different to different people. As you develop into an operator and master the fundamentals, your definition of success may change with your perception. You may relish the small wins: opening doors, having the power switched on, the furniture arriving on time, meeting a great barista ready to work for you. As you rack up the successes and deal with the challenges, stay aware of what you are celebrating and your expectations. Do you need to lower them to have more fun? Or are you itching to grow and expand, and turn your side hustle into something bigger?

If you are an alpha type personality, used to pushing your way to success, doing what you want, or micromanaging, this early stage can be challenging. As a perfectionist you can see every little problem - but you may miss the big picture and the actual game by insisting others are in the wrong.

Growing a business can be gnarly and chaotic. It takes time for a brand to establish itself, and for markets to develop awareness. The slow build is powerful, but you can't rush it. Being clearly focused on what success is to you means you can enjoy growing, securing bookings, and planning for next year. Congratulate yourself that you are selling anything. Many try and fail at this level. Success is sometimes implied through successful branding, but in reality the two are not related.

How you define success is up to you, and worth a moment's reflection and thought. What does success look like to you? Is it:

- Money in the bank?
- Bills paid on time every time?
- Building a business from your own idea?
- Symbolic - a new car, house, clothing?
- Spending more quality time with your kids or partner?
- Having time to pursue a life outside the business and cultivate yourself?
- Other people seeing you in a certain way, the way you've always wanted to be seen?
- Making a complete change from the life you've been leading?

Defining success for yourself is the first step in setting up a framework that keeps you motivated to tend to the business fundamentals, and then get on with the other important things in your life. Write down what milestones you want to reach in your business plan, and by when. Then stop and reflect after year one, and again after year two. It really is a great feeling to watch something grow as a consequence of your attention, investment and consistent care.

Unavoidable actions

Sometimes we forget what we are doing and who we are doing it for at a very basic level. If you are not used to being in business or treat the tourism venture as a hobby, it's easy to develop quirks or overindulge in areas that are not essential for success, that can eat up profits, set up incorrect expectations, and create disappointment for owner and customer alike. I see this blind spot often when my clients are talking about wanting growth, but have little insight into weaknesses that are apparent to their visitors.

In any discipline, you will hear teachers say that ten minutes of practise every day on the basics will improve muscle memory and performance. Footwork if you are a dancer, the scales if you are a musician, pedal time if you are a cyclist.

Tip: Revisiting your website, upgrading your prices, planning some social posts, making a few phone calls to introduce yourself to a regional tourism manager or local industry operator, upskilling in a new area each year – these are the equivalent of ten minutes daily practice in tourism.

Anything that requires skill requires practise, and it will come over time, but you do need to put the time in, although sometimes it will feel overwhelming. But that is when you need to do it. You are capable of many things - more than you may think right now. Believe me, it will get easier as you find ways to make your business more efficient and to work for you. And as you start to get more enquiries and bookings, it will be worth it.

How long will all this take?

It took me four years of continual questioning and many brain-frying deep dives in the ATO website, not to mention conversations with my accountant, to wrap my head around GST and PAYG, adjustments, deadlines, and cashflow. I now run two businesses as a self-taught entrepreneur, and my MBA did not prepare me for the long task lists and constant action required. Then Xero software became available, and this was a game changer in terms of bookkeeping. It was so much faster to manage and track bills, invoices, bookings, and costs - and my habits are now so ingrained that I can do other things and trust my accountant has what he needs at tax time. Here's to being adaptable in the 2020s!

Here are some fun tourism time facts. It takes:

- **30 seconds** to pour a glass of wine
- **5 minutes** to check your Instagram, Facebook and LinkedIn feeds to make sure you have not missed too much action
- **10 minutes** to meditate and set yourself up for the day and/or night
- **One day** to apply for an ABN and establish a business legally
- **One to two years** to have a set of accounts that you can use to demonstrate trade and apply for grants
- **Two years** to be out of start-up phase, although this can go on for more
- **Three years** to be accepted by old school export agents as established in international markets
- **But one day** to enter export markets if you use an online travel agent (OTA), or roughly 8-12 months if you are using domestic travel agents and inbounders for them to get to know you and do their due diligence
- **Up to three years,** sometimes less, to have a new business brand established and accepted in the market by agents, STOs and trade referral partners

As you get more serious as an operator (see Chapter 7), you will need to dedicate between half-a-day and a day a week to business administration such as responding to Council requests for site inspections, renewing insurance, marketing, proactive follow-ups, ideas, and reflection/analysis with someone trusted and objective about what you are doing, reviewing your pricing, developing new products, doing maintenance, and talking to your staff. It is all essential.

My key message in this book is to focus on core principals as the basis and groundwork of future success. You will always have ups and downs in bookings, and early on bookings may be few and far between. By doing the essentials well and consistently, you will be amazed at just how successful your regional tourism business becomes. And in three to five years, you may be in a position to grab an opportunity when it arises and reinvest. If you have already done all this, by making just a few tweaks now you won't have to backtrack to implement something from scratch, and you'll be better able to take advantage of opportunities.

What are the fundamentals?

- Do you know what your monthly costs are?
- Are you making enough money to cover your costs and then some?
- Do you charge enough?
- Are you comfortable with your price?
- Do you know what good bookings look like in your industry sector at your size and level?
- Do you have a bookings or occupancy goal each year that reflects some growth as your brand becomes known over time?
- Have you defined what is under your control and what's out of your control (see list)?
- Do you know what your bread and butter market is, and are you doing what it takes to keep it satisfied?
- Are you keeping your costs to a minimum without scrimping?
- Do you have a positive attitude, demonstrate you love what you do, and welcome people to look around your business?
- Are you looking after your staff, including superannuation and paying your cleaner and front-facing staff industry rates or more so that you can call on them in an emergency, and rely on them to manage the business if you are suddenly away or sick?
- Are your brand and service popping up where they will be seen by the right people?
- Have you taken great photos that don't over-embellish or over-promise – the actual experience that people will have (and agree they have had)?
- Do you upgrade sheets and towels, replace breakages, update the yard and signage, and carry out maintenance often enough?
- Do you have an outlet for direct customer feedback so you can address and objectively track complaints and what is working well?
- Are you on ATDW? Yes, it's a marketing thing (but not the only thing), meaning you officially exist for aggregate website tourism data trawlers
- Do you give consistent, practical instructions to your guests that they read?
- Do you respond to enquiries and bookings within 12-24 hours?
- Do you take some time out to work with other operators in your street, town, region?
- Do you have a great easy-to-find-and-navigate website that shows what people can experience, book, and pay for online?

Now, that's my kind of checklist.

Quick Lessons

Less is more

Generally a well thought out experience leaves lots of room for a customer to cruise through seamlessly - I call this the less is more principle. It doesn't mean do less, it means think about all elements of your offering more, and make strategic decisions to leave things out. For example:

- Complex colour schemes
- Over-servicing or mollycoddling adults who can find the toilets and get their own coffee without help
- Excessive small print contracts and insurance waivers right before the tour starts. Mood killer!
- Non-essential steps in a process
- Charging extra for Wi-Fi

There is a psychological landscape travellers can get into – you may know it, if you have lived out of a suitcase. You let go of all the trappings, and you appreciate the simple things. There is more space for new thoughts, ideas. Your life is uncomplicated by choices that you need to drive. You have the essential things - a phone charger, a comfortable bed, clean clothes, transport, food, and a nice room with a good view, a tasty meal, and great service. Most people are happy if they tick these boxes.

Adopt a minimalist approach. Leave out all the non-essentials and clutter. All the things you leave out are what make the space and time for something new.

Another way to deliver minimalism is by reducing friction in the customer experience (or CX). Generally tourism businesses fall into a high-servicing and contact/very tailored experience, or low-service and low friction. Consider the vital touch points of a visitor's experience at your place of business. A seamless booking and check-in process is a way to achieve this before tourists arrive, adding to the perception that if everything is this easy, it's going to be great! First online impressions matter.

You want to eliminate friction in transactions, so having standard automated responses post-booking not only saves time (you will send out hundreds of these, so automate early), but reassures guests that you've covered all the basics: how to get here, and what to bring and expect. Again, less is more, so keep instructions simple. Most people only read 20% of what you write anyway.

Set it up once, and sell it over and over again

Many operators give into the temptation, especially in accommodation where design plays a big part, to fuss over details - the coffee cups, the cutlery, the right lighting. The discipline in a regional tourism business is to set things up for success, and when it works and no one complains then it is not an issue. It's working, so leave it alone, and don't fix it if it ain't broke. The experience is enough. You need to trust this, and not overdeliver.

Leisure travellers are mostly an independent bunch - but again it depends on your target market. A key to profitability is knowing when enough is enough, and not to overinvest - keep your money in your pocket for another business, a holiday of your own.

Accommodation

When you design your accommodation or a gathering space in an attraction, I recommend working with 'good bones'. Here are my top eight tips:

1. You want to set up the entrance well - the garden, the gates, the front door, the hallway
2. Do you have good natural light, a room feature you can play with?
3. Update the paintwork or woodwork every 5-7 years with a neutral palette and some feature walls that are not garish
4. Invest in quality sheets and towels, and the best mattresses you can afford - I go medium hard as they do soften over time. People always comment on whether the beds are good or bad
5. A good couch or collective sitting area - not too ritzy as you want people to be able to relax, not feel like they are in a show room
6. Mood lighting for the living or shared spaces - there are lots of affordable, interesting mood lights at IKEA or Freedom these days
7. Purchase unique local artwork that reflects the region to hang on the walls. Don't go for anything generic. People appreciate something 'on-brand', as it helps them stay in being somewhere else mode, and being on holiday - the allure of travel
8. Airflow. Make sure there are no nasty, musty smells of old woodsmoke, the last guest's perfume or tikka masala in the microwave, cigarette smoke or rubbish not taken out soon enough. Air your rooms regularly

If you do just these things in a region where there are few accommodation options, you can sell that experience over and over again for $160 a night, paying off a $4,000 upgrade in 25 nights. That's less than a month.

Tours

For a tour, make sure:

- The vehicle is clean, newish, no bumps or dings, and well signed, windows clean and seatbelts working
- Audio - ensure people can hear your driver with a proper microphone if they are in a bus or a noisy 4WD
- As a tour operator, the transfer is critical. Where you pick the guests up and drop them off is also part of the experience. Don't just leave guests on a street corner without directions
- Have a map to show people where they are if you are off the grid and in a remote or natural setting, or if the demographic is more familiar give them a paper map. If it works, use it!

A facilitated handover to the hotel/restaurant/tour host is a free gesture that adds a lot of value. It shows that:

- You care
- You know people in the industry, and can vouch for them
- That you are reliable and trustworthy
- Worth the money they have spent

Attractions

This principle, applied to attractions, is straightforward. Earlier I gave the numbers for an attraction such as a gallery space like MONA, but it also applies to a music or dance performance, a festival with an entry price, and a National Park charging per vehicle for a day's visit. There are hours, days, weeks and years of work in a performance, a curated art show, a new building, an old-growth forest.

Whatever the attraction is, set it up well:

- Engage a curator to help you plan, design and think through the story and the visitor experience
- Partner with other businesses to share the overheads to keep costs down and more foot traffic coming

- Don't neglect the parking, the rest rooms, the café and bar – or any of the peripheral but still important amenities
- Think through the timing of on-site events, the music, and lighting
- Ensure accessibility for people living with disabilities and using wheels to get around. Also people with vision problems or hearing aids and, increasingly, young people on the spectrum, who may not deal well with noise, flickering lights or crowds
- Work out your entrance price and consider ticketing for an hour, a day, the weekend, or a season ticket, and keep it free for the locals as a way to bring in VFRs

Then sell it over and over again to keep a steady stream coming in.

Give people what they want (before they have to ask for it)

We've all seen it - the business owner scrimping and saving, and making it hard for customers to get what they need. Sugar is behind the counter, please ask for it. Paying by credit card will incur a $2 charge on top of the transaction. It's petty and creates frustration. You want to reduce friction and make it easy for your customer.

If people want to celebrate the end of their tour with a photograph and a beer, then pack the esky and get it done. Don't charge them all $5 extra per beer and make it hard to pay by only taking cash. Add it into the cost of the tour/room when they are booking or, better still, add it to the ticket price at the start. It's foresight people appreciate, and it shows your professionalism. As an operator, you should be able to pre-empt what they want and need, so when you offer it at booking they say yes. It could be a packed lunch, a transfer, breakfast - whatever extras you are able to offer, supply with grace, and make a margin on.

Wi-Fi ? Why not!

Ample free Wi-Fi and great coffee and tea are the two fundamentals in Australian regional tourism that you really should not be getting wrong. We are not just talking about kids gaming here - people are working on the road, staying in touch with family, sometimes in emergencies, and organising life events, which all require the Internet. If you are making people pay $10 for two hours of Wi-Fi like I had to on a work trip at an outback hotel recently, you are still in the 20th century. Not a bad place to be if you are carrying a brick phone around in your ra-ra skirt, but for modern travellers this is a big no-no. Resist being the stereotype of an outdated regional backwater. Wi-Fi is available in most places in Australia, and another $10 on top of a standard domestic plan can buy an extra 50-100GB a month, so what are you scrimping for? Just pay for it and build it into your nightly rate. Simple as that. If you need to stand out for something, let it be unlimited Wi-Fi and excellent coffee, and raise your rate by $10 a night, get more bookings, and pay for a coffee maker and an unlimited plan that are both tax deductible, costing you effectively nothing.

Being a tight ass has its place

On the other hand, keeping tight control over your expenses is not a bad thing. In fact it's kind of elemental in making money. There are now plenty of cheap ways to feed people, and to furnish a house or small hotel in funky colours with modern furniture without spending a fortune. But creating dramas at or after the point of purchase is not cool. Chasing $10 here and there for extra Wi-Fi or an extra blanket, well, forgeddaboudit! My friend, you are thinking too small.

If things are so tight, perhaps you are not charging enough or investing enough in the market that can afford to pay. Undercharging is a sure way not to succeed. As soon as a competitor opens, you will lose custom if you've made it too hard. Often this kind of scrimping is a result of minimal competition in a market where the bar is set low, ready for the taking.

Be ready to spend money to make money

This may sound contradictory, but you do need to upgrade at some point. A new car, vehicle, uniform, furnishings. My general rule of thumb is to invest 20% of my profit in a new capital item or product development and expect to get a return on that in 2-3 years by increasing my rates a bit and keeping the market's attention on my business by offering something new – all things being equal, which you can only pray for given the volatility in tourism.

Frictionless is fantastic

Representing the modern world in your patch - even if you are living under a rock or underground as in the case of Coober Pedy – and having mod-cons on tap is not a sell-out. First you will stand out because chances are no one else is doing it. But modern travellers expect and enjoy easy access, a good meal, and fast, simple check in and out. Don't fuss over small, unnecessary things. Leave guests alone to get on with their experience. Reduce unnecessary transactions that eat into your time. Systems that provide frictionless service are: Paywave, online check-in, links for reviews, advance SMS reminders, and auto keypad entry.

Feel the fear and let me hear you say yes!

Your reptilian brain does not get to make the big calls. It can have input - don't worry, it will - but make sure it does not drive the car. You do. Your ideas do, your intelligence, and your energy. You can manage your emotions and master your mind. If you cover the basics well, and have spent time thinking about what people really need and want as the essentials of your product, tour or service, then you have done the heavy lifting. Still, you may be worrying about your new venture. This is the risk element. It is visceral and your brain is screaming at you to just woah nelly and stop right there! You be crazy?

I used to think, would people like it? Was it enough? Would anyone book me in the summer? Would they manage without being hosted? Could I let go enough to let it happen without me? Would I really make money like that?

The answer is yes.

Yes. Yes it was. They did. They still do. Yes, I can, and yes, I do. Amen.

Underpromise and overdeliver

Putting yourself out there can be nerve-wracking until you realise you are succeeding. Or at least not failing. A strategy I used to reduce my risk was to offer whatever I could, but not talk it up, an underpromise, overdeliver approach that gave customers the opportunity to have their own experience, and then comment and let others - and me - know how they found it. They loved it. And then I worked out - ok, I can have a bit more confidence this is working now, and that's what I can sustainably manage from a remote location. Being remote, I can't respond instantly to every whim and need, so I'm literally at arm's length, and I say upfront the house is for independent adventurers, and I proactively manage how I want them to engage with me.

Customer service is not free

While it's free to be kind and smile and be a good person and all that jazz, customer service is a cost to any business, often hidden or overlooked. A smile is free, but if you have to do it all day every day, you know it is not far from a snarl. Still, people want service and businesses have found cheaper ways of providing it en masse with personalised tech, so I suggest you embrace this as much and as soon as possible. Automate customer service where you can without being a total robot. Efficiency is where you compete, gain and simplify behind the scenes processes to keep it easy for you and your customers. Specifically, I refer to booking and reservation systems, calendar availability, directions and mapping, and other pre- and post-visit communications that give assurances you are ready for your next very unique and special guest.

After many years, I now cut my losses and rarely return calls for direct enquiries who haven't done their background. The 5% who call will take 20% of my time, and even then there's no guarantee they'll book and pay. Working outside an automated booking process costs me time I don't have to check up on payments, reconcile, and follow up. I'm just not set up that way in my small accommodation business.

If you run a tour or an attraction, there's no getting away from it - you are front line with customers, but still you want to keep the best of yourself for the people who have paid and are committed to the experience you or your team deliver.

The rule of thumb is most people can follow instructions, but occasionally someone really struggles or needs help - older people, parents with children in tow, disability access - and they need to speak to a human, to sound you out and feel secure. So speak to them, help them out if you can - not everyone is a computer whizz. Save your time for the people who really need it.

Kmart is your friend

Related to being a tight-ass, and spending money to make money, and keep it simple, Kmart is your friend. It is for those of us wanna-be interior designers who can make a space look great on a shoestring, and those of us who have no idea about design at all. Kmart is your friend because basics are basics in everyone's language, and you will be back and forth to Cheap As Chips, Kmart and/or Big W often as you replace things and upgrade your business, accommodation, café, hotel rooms, or shared BBQ areas and huts, etc.

These days, good, cheap and well-designed homewares are everywhere and readily accessible. There is no excuse for using old vegemite jars. Even if grandpa has a nice old wardrobe in the shed he's been meaning to get rid of for 20 years, it doesn't mean you should take it. It's not often a hotel wardrobe actually gets used. It's enough to have a hanging rack or a chest of drawers for the odd jacket or dress.

If you are successful, you are likely to be turning over a lot of paying guests with back-to-back bookings in peak times. In practical terms, this means things break all the time. Your cleaner is key here, telling you what's missing, and what's broken. It needs to be easy and fast to get in and clean and get out before the next guests arrive, often within hours of the last guests leaving. So you need to be able to buy similar stuff over and over again, or make it affordable to upgrade a whole set when the time comes. While you like fancy tea towels at home, these will go walking in your business. Nice stuff goes missing - humans steal, lie and make a mess. They bring their dogs, shoot their guns in your yard, and bring all their bad habits on the road (yep, I've hosted that guy). So make things nice, but cheap to replace, unattractive to steal, and you are keeping costs down by having to worry less if you do need to replace them.

Do it with style

There is a whole book I can write about styling, but my rules of thumb are:

- **Keep it simple.** Choose one colour and go with different tones and hues
- **If in doubt, choose a neutral** like tan, beige, black/white or grey. And gold or silver or copper - wood or metal. And then buy everything you can in this colour scheme or along this palette
- **Buy big mirrors** to make a space look instantly larger and more open, lighter, and more modern
- **Cover all naked lightbulbs** with a funky lampshade that throws shadows
- **Replace fluros** with dimmable downlights
- **Make sure all cooking areas are easy to clean.** It's worth doing a renovation if you have an old, tired kitchen, or at least painting the drawers all the same colour with some new handles is a good makeover if you are short of cash
- **Have one statement piece** per room, no more

Kmart and IKEA, if you have one close by, are great for kitchen pots and pans, cheap glasses, and funky plates, but buy neutral colours as you may not get that pattern again when it's time to upgrade. Sheets and towels too.

I buy greys and cream colours, and dark towels, but other people buy white and bleach regularly. Personally, I keep things as low chemical as possible, and like recycling - you can buy great second-hand furniture in and around your region on Facebook Marketplace or local Buy, Swap, Sell Facebook Groups. That will save you a 20-week wait for a new couch (plus regional delivery rates - no thanks!), plus give your accommodation a comfortable lived-in feel, and not a squeaky vibe that also says new and maybe not that popular.

While I'm a fan of recycling for the same reasons, you want a set of a minimum of four of everything that is hard-wearing and can be put in a dishwasher, solid oven proof dishes and cutting boards. Most people don't bake on holiday... they just find a pub, but I've had occasional guests who do want a lamb roast, so it does happen. Your job is not to judge who on earth would cook a roast on holiday, but to buy a $7 baking dish and some oven cleaner for later, and give them what they want.

Diversity is the new normal

If you find yourself cringing over a reservation or booking or starting to nitpick why you won't let someone stay, take a deep breath. Of course you have the right to refuse. It's your business, and sometimes someone may be pushing the limits, disrespectful, or just giving the wrong signals or attitude. But it is illegal in Australia to discriminate against someone based on race, sexual orientation or just plain you-made-it-up. You need to have grounds for saying no or refusing someone. If you do say no without good reason, people remember and talk, and this can affect market perception, even if you can't see it happen or you are justified.

Are you or is your customer the only gay in the village?

Regional and country Australia does not have a great reputation for being a friendly place to the LGBTQI community. Country people can be conservative and feel threatened by new or different people. Many queer folks escaped regional towns growing up to find freedom and acceptance in larger cities. So if you and your town make an effort to welcome the Lesbian, Gay, Bisexual, Trans, Queer, Intersex markets, and overcome barriers with welcoming marketing, you can differentiate yourself and attract bookings from a loyal customer base. It's all about signalling to your guests that you cater to them, and they will be safe and welcomed in your space/tour/home. If you want to do more in this area to attract travellers, check out the useful resources at the end of this chapter.

To be truly welcoming to all types, you can be overt or subtle. Fly the rainbow flag on your window or website. As a standard procedure ask all your guests at booking to confirm in writing how they would like the bed configuration and withhold any assumptions or judgements. The truth is, we don't need to know who's sleeping where, or with whom to take a booking and run a business. It's simply not important. A booking is a booking. Your cleaner just needs to know how many beds to make up, your receptionist needs to stay calm when two men check into a queen room, and your tour guide must not gawp when two women cuddle on the back seat. The world will keep turning.

If you are in tourism and this section is challenging for you in any way, I gently suggest you explore your unconscious beliefs, where they come from, and own your own prejudice. Take action here. Not everyone grew up with queer or multicultural friends and family, so it may not be easy for you to accept people who are different to you, but it's the 21st century and you are in the tourism industry. It's all about people and diversity and choice.

A booking is a booking

You want to be booked out. This is the goal if you have a lot of beds, capacity and tour seats: places to fill every day. Despite having target markets and homing in, you may get bookings from all over the place. It's also worth considering new markets no one else caters to or which are too hard for many people. There are few people I know in business who refuse money unless they are already booked out.

Fake it till you make it

Who knows what you can do until you are asked, or until you try? Can you accommodate a football team's Premiership Dinner in your regional restaurant or pub? Can you host a film crew for two weeks? Can someone leave their caravan in your shed for a week's rent while they 4WD an inaccessible part of the region? Can you hire out your yard for a native plant workshop or a cooking demonstration as part of a regional Food and Wine Festival event? If you have the structure in place, sometimes these left field enquiries can be interesting and creative ways to get more exposure to people who might not have ever come on their own - and will be pleasantly surprised, and maybe return and tell their friends. Say yes, and then work it out on the way through. I can't tell you how many business people I know who laugh and nod when this comes up - we all do it.

Business is essentially creative. You must be flexible, come up with ideas and make stuff work if you are taking money. That's the deal. So if you don't know how, fake it until you do!

Case Study 3

Build it and they will come

I worked with an inbound bookings specialist to help an established NT outback tour operator, Emu Run Experience, to tap into a new export backpacker market.

No stranger to international markets, Emu Run was booking hundreds of travellers from all over the world already in Australia wanting to visit Uluru. The strategy was to get bookings before people arrived in Australia to secure a market and not compete locally for last-minute business.

Like many operators new to exporting, my client resisted paying a 30% commission to agents in the UK, Europe and the USA without a guarantee of volume - and rightly so - that's a lot of money to hand over for one or two bookings, and he needed to fill buses.

Korea was then an emerging economy. In the late 2010s, not many operators in the NT were targeting Asian markets; it was considered a bit too hard, and just wasn't being done. Lots of Chinese bus tours dominated Sydney, and the assumption was they weren't interested in the outback experience. We thought Korea was a good option to dip a toe in the water - huge volume, low cost to enter, commissions were negotiable, and many Korean students were in Australia at the time so family could visit. It was a new market for the outback.

My inbound colleague said, when I wondered if the client would respond, "He's running a business isn't he? A booking is a booking, no matter where it comes from. If he's covering costs and making a margin after commissions, he's making money."

I never forgot that. Money is money and a booking is a booking.

The client agreed to the strategy, and pursued the Korean backpacker market. He settled on a good commission rate, lower than traditional UK and European agents would charge. Patrick built a language app, had marketing materials translated, got in-bus Wi-Fi so guests could post and hashtag their hearts out back home, and trained his guides to work with Korean market behaviours such as food and camping and bedding preferences. He invested in attending tradeshows and followed up with phone calls to win bookings, and they started to trickle in. He opened up a crack that turned into a chasm, taking him from second in the Central Australian tour industry to number one, and the only provider to Korean markets at the time.

There are millions of Koreans studying, living and working in Australia, and their families come and visit, and want to see Uluru. Their money is as good as anyone's. Now he has market loyalty as a first mover in a whole new market.

Let's summarise

- What does success look like to you? How you define success will change as you grow, but make it conscious so you can enjoy the journey and know when you have achieved it - then celebrate!
- There are unavoidable pressures in running a business, and new skills require practise. Make a habit of getting out of your operations to build your network and digital skills, and update your marketing for 15 minutes a day
- Less is more: if in doubt, do less and keep design and messages simple, colours neutral, and items like crockery plain and replaceable
- Set it up well, and sell it over and over - this is the essence of a good business: making money from capital to get a return on investment
- Don't be stingy. Give people what they want, and make it easy for them to book and pay for Wi-Fi, add-ons, and basics
- A booking is a booking, and there are many diverse markets which want to travel, and many people new to your region will love what you have to offer
- LGTBQI travellers are looking for safe places to travel and spend their time and money. Understand their experiences and how you can make their check-in, stay, and check-out something to write home about - in a good way

Hollow Mountain, Grampians National Park. Visit Victoria

LET'S CONNECT AND GET YOU ON THE ROAD

If you like what you've read and are looking for ways to stay inspired and keep ideas flowing in your regional tourism business, why not stay in touch?

Here are some of the ways to contact me. I love hearing from readers and tourism operators everywhere.

You are not alone.

Connect with me on

Linked In: www.linkedin.com/in/susan-lee-cvc

Instagram: www.instagram.com/cvcadviser

Facebook: www.facebook.com/cvcadviser

Subscribe to our eNews at **www.cvconsult.com.au**

Check out the free Booked Out! resources at **https://cvconsult.com.au/bookedout-resources** for worksheets, research, short videos and interviews

THE BOOKED OUT! TOURISM PROGRAM™

It's often hard to find good support in regions, making professional development programs rare for anyone with a serious interest in a tourism career. Booked Out! Tourism Programs are tailored for regional tourism and economic development professionals, Indigenous entrepreneurs and small business owners anywhere in Australia. Invest in yourself or your team and learn the essential business skills to succeed in the sector. Your knowledge and networks are your biggest asset, so it makes sense to invest in one of our programs. Meet like-minded peers across Australia. Plus it's tax deductible. Win!

Booked Out! Tourism Capacity Building Program

The Booked Out Tourism Program™ is a short intensive for anyone wanting to increase their knowledge of regional tourism and tourism business growth. In small groups over a number of weeks we work through key concepts covered in this book to build your knowledge, skills and capacity. Perfect for tourism professionals in business, local government, regional development, Indigenous start ups and staff in regional tourism attractions, tours and accommodation, anywhere in Australia.

Tourism Business Adviser Program

If you are looking for a more intensive, focused approach, The Tourism Business Adviser Program ™ is for you. Work one on one with Susan Lee to plan and start your tourism attraction, tour or accommodation. You get a 12 month program of tailored support and access to Susan's industry network to take your business from idea to 'hello bookings!' Be guided by the leading industry expert at your own pace, using worksheets, tools and direct coaching and support, and by the end of the year you will be delighted as your business and confidence flourish.

Enquire online at **www.cvconsult.com.au/bookedout-buy**

Tasman Peninsula Waves, South East Tasmania. Photo by Alastair Bett

ACRONYMS

FIT	Free Independent Traveller	RDA	Regional Development Australia	TIC	Tourism Industry Council
VFR	Visiting Friends and Relatives	OTA	Online Travel Agent	HVT	HIgh Value Traveller
STO	State Tourism Organisation	SME	Small and Medium Enterprise	NVS	National Visitor Survey
IVS	International Visitor Survey	ITO	Inbound Tour Operator	ABN	Australian Business Number
RTA/RTO	Regional Tourism Association or Organisation	ABR	Australian Business Register	VIC	Visitor Information Centre
LTA/LTO/ LGTA	Local Tourism Association/ Organisation or Local Government Tourism Association	4WD	Four wheel driver	TRA	Tourism Research Australia
LGBTQI	Lesbian Gay Bisexual Transgender Queer and Intersex	TA	Tourism Australia	NIAA	National Indigenous Australians Agency
IBA	Indigenous Business Australia	IOB	Indigenous owned business	MICE	Meetings Incentives Conferences Events
NAIDOC	National Aborigines and Islanders Day Observance Committee	FIFO	Fly in, fly out	PAYG	Pay As You Go

Resources by Chapter

Resources mentioned in this book are available for download at the CVC Clear Vision Consulting website **https://cvconsult.com.au/bookedout-resources**.

Chapter 1

- Tourism Research Australia Australian tourism region data profiles https://www.tra.gov.au/regional/tourism-region-profiles/tourism-regional-profiles
- Guide to starting a business https://business.gov.au/Guide/Starting
- Business Registration Service https://register.business.gov.au/
- ASIC https://asic.gov.au/
- Australian Business Registrar Applying for an ABN https://www.abr.gov.au/business-super-funds-charities/applying-abn

Chapter 2

- Resources - Clear Vision Consulting https://cvconsult.com.au/resources
- BNI - Chapter Map http://events.bni.com.au/en-AU/findachapter
- Find your Chamber here Australian Chamber of Commerce and Industry https://www.australianchamber.com.au/
- Mark Bouris What it Takes, How to Work in Business by Mark Bouris https://www.booktopia.com.au/what-it-takes-mark-bouris/book/9781741756852.html
- How to Network - Learn to Love Networking https://hbr.org/2016/05/learn-to-love-networking

Chapter 3

- Find your local council here - Local Government Association https://alga.com.au/resources/local-government-associations/
- Tourism Australia Signature Experiences Program Signature Experiences of Australia - Corporate https://www.tourism.australia.com/en/resources/industry-resources/industry-programs/signature-experiences-of-australia.html
- Tourism Industry Council of Australia https://www.facebook.com/AustralianTIC/
- United Nations Sustainable Development Goals (SDGs) https://sdgs.un.org/goals

Chapter 4

- Australian Tourism Accreditation Program - Quality Tourism Australia https://www.qualitytourismaustralia.com/australian-tourism-accreditation-program/
- Tourism Awards https://www.qualitytourismaustralia.com/australian-tourism-awards
- ATDW https://atdw.com.au/about-us/
- Squarespace https://www.squarespace.com/
- Wix https://www.wix.com/
- Airbnb https://www.Airbnb.com.au/
- Rezdy https://rezdy.com/
- Canva https://www.canva.com/
- Distribution systems What is a Global Distribution System? https://www.youtube.com/watch?v=xF1OGj2MIEw
- Travefy software Travefy 10-Minute Demo https://youtu.be/4idxbs-lu_8
- Tourism Infrastructure Advisory https://cvconsult.com.au/tourism%20infrastructure%20advisory

Chapter 5

- Deep Breathing Exercises for Beginners https://www.youtube.com/watch?v=acUZdGd_3Dg
- Wim Hof Method Guided Breathing for Beginners (3 Rounds Slow Pace) https://youtu.be/0BNejY1e9ik
- Eco Certification | Ecotourism Australia https://www.ecotourism.org.au/our-certification-programs/eco-certification

Chapter 6

- The 5 Es worksheet Resources - Clear Vision Consulting https://cvconsult.com.au/resources
- DIY Destination Audit Resources - Clear Vision Consulting https://cvconsult.com.au/resources
- Get More Action in Your Attraction https://www.linkedin.com/pulse/activating-attractions-susan-lee/

Chapter 7

- Supply Nation https://supplynation.org.au
- Office of the Registrar of Indigenous Corporations https://www.oric.gov.au/
- National Indigenous Australians Agency https://www.niaa.gov.au/
- Indigenous Business Australia https://iba.gov.au/
- Indigenous Land and Sea Corporation https://www.ilsc.gov.au
- Indigenous Procurement Policy https://www.niaa.gov.au/indigenous-affairs/economic-development/indigenous-procurement-policy-ipp
- Desart https://desart.com.au
- Etsy Australia https://www.etsy.com/au

Chapter 8

- Christopher Vogler and The Hero's Journey... The Outline, Archetypes and Mythical Memo - Chris Jones Filmmaker Blog https://chrisjonesblog.com/2017/05/christopher-vogler-and-the-heros-journey-the-outline-archetypes-and-mythical-memo.html

Chapter 9

- Bernard Salt A.M. https://www.bernard-salt.com.au/

Chapter 10

- Visit Gay Australia https://www.visitgayaustralia.com.au/
- How to Improve LGBT Tourism Marketing Efforts, According to a City That Knows https://skift.com/2015/07/01/how-to-improve-lgbt-tourism-marketing-efforts-according-to-a-city-that-knows/
- International Gay and Lesbian Tourism Alliance IGLTA https://www.iglta.org/

Farmland at Yarragon, West Gippsland. Visit Victoria

www.ingramcontent.com/pod-product-compliance
Lightning Source LLC
LaVergne TN
LVHW071212210926
848482LV00015B/790